MW00931416

# Cesar Millan Doesn't Live Here

## The Comedy and Chaos of Living with Four Dogs

MICHELLE BROOKS

authorHOUSE®

*AuthorHouse*™
*1663 Liberty Drive, Suite 200*
*Bloomington, IN 47403*
*www.authorhouse.com*
*Phone: 1-800-839-8640*

*First published by AuthorHouse  3/24/2009*

*ISBN: 978-1-4389-5091-4 (sc)*
*ISBN: 978-1-4389-5090-7 (hc)*

*Printed in the United States of America*
*Bloomington, Indiana*

*This book is printed on acid-free paper.*

# ACKNOWLEDGMENTS AND ETERNAL GRATITUDE:

Jason: for understanding my passion for our dogs and would lay in traffic for all of us. For allowing my indulgences, my neuroses, and at times my meltdowns all the while you are supportive and sane. I truly love you. Maureen: Buttercup, you get it. I am eternally grateful for your support, insight, opinions, and assurance I am not the only one who rises and sleeps for the comfort of my dogs. Dr. Dutton, Dr. Barlow, and the staff at Weare Animal Hospital: for giving me the opportunity to be a part of your team, always squeezing me in when one of my dogs is clearly in need of some major organ transplant, understanding the intensity of my love for my pets, and your compassion when I'm scared and assuming the worst. Jen: Thank you for all the reiki. I sing your praises for Zen with Jen. Dr. Kristi Zimmerman: For always allowing me to dance on the line of insanity but reeling me in when I cross over into the world of lunacy over the dogs. Everyone at the Canine Fence Company: for allowing me to live my dream of working with dogs and calling those snow days so I can snuggle in my jammies on my couch with my dogs, and for those of you in Service Control for still being nice to me when I call in spewing potty words my mother never taught me to use. Mr.

Ken Hollingsworth, Mr. Ken Didsbury, and Mr. Mike Landroche: You uncovered my passion for writing and have you all to thank for always pushing me to do better, write from the heart, and never use the passive voice. Dr. William Fulmer: for inspiring my animation as a source of education for others. Delynn: My Moostah, this was your idea. I admire your strength, your sense of humor, and am forever grateful for all your support and laughter. Colleen: I am humbled by all your dedication to saving those who do not have a voice. I may not answer the phone every time you call, but your friendship means more to me than you know. Carol & Art Landry: for always offering solutions to our sometimes dysfunctional little Family. My parents: A child should always grow up with a furry best friend. Thank you. Mom: Thank you for always being there to take the dogs; let them out or just be a sounding board. Dad: You always come through for me and our time at the lake is very special to me. Thank you. My Dear Sweet Brother Noompsie also known as Mike: You always drop everything to help me with the dogs. Thank you. Olive Juice. Fran and Donna: For feeding us and always coming to my rescue in a crisis. The rest of my family: Words can't express my gratitude for all you do for my furry family and me. Holly: Because dear God if you weren't mentioned you'd show up and beat me with those implants. Thank you for all your generosity. I LOVE YOU CHUNK! To my Girls: Wendy, Julie, Courtney, Elby, Amy, Cindy: It's rare to have so many friends withstand the test of time like us. I love you all. Killian, Aurora, Tatum Belle, and Porter: My angels on earth. I love you. Denali: My angel watching over me. You are missed every day. Arno: My first true love.

# THE BEGINNING

The idea for this book came from one of my latest rants about how my dogs, someone or something, had crossed my path and pissed me off. Many friends had suggested I document and publish these rants, or at least have my own reality show because I'm "cute when I'm mad." It was the latest suggestion from my friend Delynn that really resonated in my heart that this could be a fun project. I am notorious for leaving long-winded, yet colorful voicemails or incredibly descriptive e-mails about the latest travesty to befall me, or apparently I have nothing better to whine about dissertation. On occasion, Jason will forward these voicemail rants to his boss just so his boss will have an appreciation of what Jason's daily life is like. By all accounts, I'm still high strung, but in my mind, I'm fairly even keeled. The best advice I can give is if you feel you need to send frequent angry updates, you're not happy. Do what makes you happy. For me, it's being able to work with dogs every day. Don't get me wrong, I have my moments where I've dealt with dogs that have no manners all day and cover me in bruises from jumping and lunging at me whose owners think that's adorable and then I lose my mind when I use a bathroom that has 1 ply toilet paper because my patience has been pushed to the limit. That being said, even at the end of a trying day, there is nothing better in my world than the love and devotion I get when I walk through the door and have four eager faces waiting to greet me because eight hours away from their mom is seven hours and fifty nine minutes too long... Well, and maybe 3 ply toilet paper, but for the most part it's about my dogs. This book is a recollection of those moments.

   Let it be known I would be a pediatrician's worst nightmare. For those pediatricians in the audience, be glad I didn't have children, as you too would be on my speed dial and number one in my e-mail address book. Until the end of time, I will be infinitely grateful to Dr. Dutton and the staff at Weare Animal Hospital for their endless patience with me. Between my mother being a nurse who waited until I was knocking on death's door to bring me to the doctor, and my brief time as a veterinary technician where diarrhea could indeed be a symptom of cancer, I have just enough information to be dangerous and I am a nervous dog mom. For most people, they will wait until their dogs (or cats) are visibly urinating blood to run a urinalysis to check for a urinary tract infection. Not me. If my dogs go pee too many times in a day, I get suspicious. That suspicion leads to the worst-case scenario play by play in my mind. That will then be followed by a phone call to my friend Maureen who also used to be a veterinarian technician and her world also rises and sets on her dogs. She will then concur the dog is clearly in kidney failure and we need to notify the transplant team to get a donor, stat, but at the very least, bring in a urine sample and perhaps a course of antibiotics. To this day, my parents are baffled at how they raised me to be so normal in most aspects, yet such a neurotic freak show about the care of my dogs. One example would be everyone was going out on the boat one glorious summer day and a friend asked if Killian could go. I didn't bring his life jacket so of course, the answer was no. Everyone, except Jason, was truly astonished that not only did he have a life jacket, but that I wouldn't make an exception to my rule… Just this once. What if he fell off the boat? He has black fur. No one would see him. Another boat could come along before we were able to get back to him and run him over killing him. Suddenly, *just this once,* has now turned into a tragedy that could include me jumping off a bridge.

However, there is also a saying in our house: If they're not broken, they're not ours. I suppose I did set us up to fail with my liberal, bleeding, and tree hugging heart. Killian was a stray dog that wandered from his home and collided with the front end of a pickup truck and shattered his pelvis, broke several teeth, and his upper lip was hanging from his face. After hitting Killian with his truck, the Good Samaritan brought Killian into the Animal Hospital where I worked at the time. Killian could barely walk, and with his upper lip was hanging in the wind from its collision with the man's grill on his truck, he was the picture of pathetic, but his eyes could melt your heart. He had a sweet "Please love me" disposition, and I was hooked. I decided to keep him and brought him home as a *surprise* gift for Jason. Being that I don't actually condone pets as gifts for anyone, it was more of a gift to me, and since Killian would be MY dog like his paycheck was actually MY money, if it would make ME happy, Jason is a very wise man and likes a happy wife and will usually roll with whatever will make me happy. To suck up though, I also brought home a six-pack of Killian's Irish Red beer as a warm him up to the "We have a dog" idea being that Killian beer was his favorite at the time and lo and behold, this little dog's name is Killian too! What are the chances? .

We adopted Aurora once the construction of our house was complete. Aurora's teeth were covered in plaque, her ears were swollen shut with infection and she had a ruptured ACL when we adopted her. Denali had a massive coronary condition and was given less than six months to live when we adopted him and he occasionally would have horrible aggression towards men that were in a fifty mile radius of me. He lived for 27 precious months. Tatum Belle developed a UTI within 36 hours of being separated from her littermates and by the time her one year birthday rolled around, she had endured 3 rounds of kennel cough, a pulled back muscle, a Staph infection with sores that covered her body, and an intestinal obstruction. Lastly, Porter was naked from his nose to his toes due to a severe case of Demodex Mange when he came to live with us and he had a confidence problem that it would often show itself as fear aggression. If they weren't broken, they weren't ours. As a result, if any symptom develops with any of the dogs, benign or otherwise, I run with the worst-case scenario and an Olympic sprinter's speed straight to my vet's office.

# The Characters

**Killian** – 12 year old Shepherd/Lab mix (also known as Baby, Punkin, and The Christ Dog)

**Aurora** – 8 year-old Bullmastiff (also known as Rora, Bora, Big Mama, and occasionally My Dainty Delicate Flower)

**Tatum Belle** – 3 year-old Pit Bull (also known as TB, Bellerina, but most commonly Beast or Imp)

**Porter** – 1 year-old Dogue de Bordeaux

**Denali** – our beloved Dogue de Bordeaux who left us all too soon at the age of four (also known as Doodles, Snoodles, Big D, D, or Snood)

**Jason** – my wonderful husband who supports every decision, including ones that include adding yet another dog to our family

# IN THE DOGHOUSE

# I'm Not Leaving My Wingman

Anyone who has more than one child (or dog) and says they don't have a favorite is lying. No really, you know who you are, and you know I'm right. But it can be our secret. I won't tell. I will openly admit, in earshot of the other dogs even, that Killian is my favorite and the reason the sun rises and sets in my world. Jason isn't joking when he says he hopes he dies before Killian does because my level of inconsolable will truly be of rubber room status and when that day comes, God forbid, there really won't be enough Valium in the world that will cover that ensuing depression.

Killian came to the Weare Animal Hospital while I was working there as a veterinary technician. He came in as a dog that had been hit by a car and wasn't wearing any identification tags, just a piece of duct tape that someone had written his name but the lettering had faded. His pelvis was shattered, his chest cavity was filled with air so his lungs couldn't expand and contract making it very difficult for him to breathe, his upper lip had been partially torn and was hanging off, and several teeth were broken. Due to his lack of apparent ownership, the protocol for the town of Weare is the Animal Control Officer has to approve any and all medical care to stray animals because if no one claims the dog, the town has to foot the bill. Killian waited almost 24 hours before we were given the approval to care for him.

However, he was by far the sweetest dog you had ever met. He never complained, and he always had the driest and gentlest kisses. When he was stable enough, I took him home to be my boy. We were inseparable. He went to work with me. He went to the store with me. He even went to the bathroom with me. He went everywhere with me. And if he wasn't welcome where I wanted to go, we simply didn't go. Oh yes, I was rapidly becoming one of "those" people. To this day, I will admit he is the monster I created.

As a result of him being my furry shadow, he has a pretty decent case of separation anxiety. When we still lived in the condominium complex, I came home one afternoon and as I was walking up the walkway to our building I heard the pitiful howl of a dog. I looked up and realized that howl was coming from our unit. As I was unlocking my door, our neighbor came out and said he had been doing that all day. Now that we are in our house, we have to open the windows from the top down because he has jumped through two of them to come find me. I have accidentally forgotten to lock his crate door and have come home to find the window grates ripped from the windowpanes, chewed doorknobs, and one very stressed dog. How could I leave him to his own accord all by himself and expect him to cope? What was I thinking? That was abandonment in its worst form, or so he thought. He's my dog, he's my monster, he loves me with blind devotion and in turn, I will set myself on fire for him.

When Jason and I were building our house, our patience, and quite honestly, our marriage, was put to many, many, many tests. Killian was there with me, providing me with a source of sanity. We sold our condominium prior to completion of our house so we were "living" on site as we built our house. Jason's mother had loaned us her camper so we had a place to potty and brush our teeth as construction progressed. Dr. Dutton allowed us to use the shower and washing machine at the Animal Hospital during the building process. Every morning before heading to the animal hospital to shower etc, Killian and I had a ritual. I would go into the camper to potty and brush my teeth. He would go do his business in the woods.

One morning during our routine, Killian had gone exploring. I came out of the camper and he was gone. Being that it was before 6:00 AM, Jason was still asleep and I didn't want to wake him by yelling "KILLIAN," I started to walk down the driveway, quietly calling to him. He wasn't anywhere to be seen or heard romping in the woods. I got to the end of our driveway, which is a quarter of a mile long, and I was now on the very busy road on which we live. Being that is was almost 6:00 AM, the morning rush hour traffic hadn't started yet, but it was going to commence in about twenty minutes and I sure didn't want my baby getting hit by a car again. On some mornings, we see as many as thirty cars go by the driveway before we are able to exit it and start our own commutes to work. I had to make a choice which way to go, so I headed to my right. A man in a red pick up truck drove by and asked if I was all right since I clearly wasn't out for a morning jog in my jeans and Teva sandals. I told him my dog had taken off and gave a brief description, my voice quivering a little. The man wished me luck and drove off.

A few minutes later, the man returned in his pick up truck saying he had seen my dog, and he would drive me to him. I assessed the situation: It's 6:00 in the morning. Jason doesn't know I'm gone. My cell phone is still on the nightstand where I had left it. I have no idea who this man is and if he isn't going to put me in a well with a bottle of lotion with a bucket like in Silence of the Lambs. At the time, I weighed 125 pounds and a strong gust of wind could have blown me away but as tough as my ego thinks it is, I know darn well any random psycho could over power me. Not to mention in the back of my head I hear my mother telling me never to get into a car with a stranger. Whatever. It's Killian and this man said he has seen him. I have a 50/50 shot of living through this and if I get my dog back, those are odds I'm willing to take. Sure enough, about a half mile down the road, my dog was eating my neighbor's begonias. I called Killian and he willingly came and hopped into the man's truck and he drove me back to the driveway. I am forever grateful for the angel who helped me find my little dog.

When we were living without power, it also meant we were living without cable. Football season had commenced for over two months now and every Sunday, I would sit in my truck and listen to the game on the radio. It wasn't the same, it wasn't even close, and I was miserable. Basically, we were living without anything that made life, as we know it, civilized. My life had felt like it had become a Dirty Jobs episode, my nerves were fried and I was on the brink of a breakdown.

The following week after Killian went wandering, we scheduled the Inspector to come check to make sure we had followed all the codes and protocol for the go ahead for turning on the power to our house. Power meant a bathroom with running water. Power meant a real alarm clock and not my cell phone that didn't have a snooze button to wake us every morning. Power meant... Well, power meant I could go shopping for a refrigerator instead of ice for the cooler to hold the food we could only buy in a supply of one day at a time since we only had one beach cooler. Power meant I might not kill Jason because somehow this is his entire fault.

Being that I worked five miles from the house, I went to meet the inspector on my lunch break. It was raining and miserable out. But Jason had promised me that we would be with power after this meeting so my spirits were high. It wasn't meant to be. I was crushed when the inspector not only told me we failed our inspection, but it would be three weeks before he could come back and check our progress.

I had no intention of playing the girl card, but I did. I had just had it with all the set backs of building a house and started crying. This poor man must not handle women crying well because he started stammering "Oh ma'am, I I I I I wish I could…" I don't know what made me blurt this out, but at that exact moment, I wasn't concerned about things like showering at home, using my own bathroom without having to go outside, cooking a dinner without using a grill, or getting a beer from a place other than a cooler. I was concerned with my dog's safety. I was in between sniffles when I cried, "I need my Invisible Fence." The inspector pulled some strings and we had power at the end of that week. We had the Invisible Fence® installed two days later. My boy was never leaving me again.

As a veterinary technician, I was entitled to a great discount on the installation of my Invisible Fence® and I also received three lessons to train Killian on how to learn and respect his boundaries so he would stay in the yard. It was the trainer who came to our house, Diana, who peaked my interest in working for the Canine Fence Company as a dog trainer.

By all accounts, the dogs are the monsters I created. I typically don't go from room to room without an entourage. I make being with me quite possibly the best thing for them. As a result, they are all fiercely loyal to me and I am finely in tune with them. It is rare when I don't know what they are thinking, and usually it's about cheese. Diana picked up on this and encouraged me to send in my resume. It was with mixed emotions and a sense of betrayal to Dr. Dutton I applied for a job with the Canine Fence Company. But not every job is for everyone and being a veterinary technician was taking its toll on my heart. I loved my job. I loved the people I worked with. That being said, one day we euthanized four dogs before 9:00 AM. The last customer had asked that I be there for her dog because she didn't have the strength to hold her paw as she died. I was taking work home with me and it was just too emotionally draining. Within a few months, I ended my career as a veterinary technician and started my career at the Canine Fence Company training dogs to the Invisible Fence®.

A couple years passed and it is now the joyous holiday season. My in laws, Jason's brother Dave and his wife Vicki, whom I truly do adore, were scheduled to arrive from Oregon the Friday afternoon before Christmas, which was on Sunday. When they are in town, the whole family makes a point to make time for Dave and Vicki. They come east every few years and being that they are pretty awesome people, everyone does want to see them. Jason and Dave are very close and always spend hours catching up so Dave and Vicki stay with us. Plus we have a pool table and we all drink like fish shooting pool til the wee hours of the night. The issue is they have so many people to see in a short time frame so the schedule is pretty tight with comings and goings. We had a full weekend of family gatherings to attend, starting the evening they arrived just two hours after their flight landed.

Four days prior to their arrival, Killian wasn't acting like himself. Monday, he was mopey. Tuesday, he wasn't keeping anything down, including water. Wednesday, he was visibly losing weight and went to see Dr. Dutton. His blood work was clear, but a preliminary x ray showed something funky in his intestinal tract. We scheduled the barium x ray series the next day to determine if Killian had an obstruction.

In the kitchen that evening, I was less than calm and bless Jason's heart, he was doing his best to comfort me. This was Killian, it was 4 days before Christmas, and I was assuming the worst. Not to mention, his vet bill was already up to $200, an upper GI barium series is going to be another $150 and then... I didn't finish my sentence; just fell into Jason's arms sobbing. He assured me the Christ Dog would be fine, we have a credit card for a reason, and of course we would fix our dog.

Thursday, Dr. Dutton called and the x rays showed barium was stuck in his stomach and the doctor felt he had an obstruction. Killian was set for surgery on Friday, two days before Christmas. That evening, I picked up Killian from the animal hospital and suddenly, it hit me. My baby was ten years old and needed major surgery. I was shaking as I filled out the Surgery Release form and since this was going on the credit card, I spared no expense. He was to receive the "good" drugs for pain management. Forget Torbutrol and Rimadyl. That's just baby aspirin in the world of pain control. I wanted my perfect little dog to have the best drugs: Morphine and a three-day Fentanyl patch. The doctor assured me he would be fine as I reminded him this wasn't any ordinary dog this was *Killian*.

I had a meeting in Connecticut Friday morning. The Home Office for the Canine Fence Company is four hours from my house and I needed to be there at 10:00 AM so I couldn't drop him off for surgery that day but had every intention of bailing early to get home to pick up my little pooch. Connecticut is a funny little state. It's illegal to talk on your cell phone and drive, even with a headset or blue tooth. Dr. Dutton called me on my cell phone after the surgery was complete with the update. Naturally, I was not only in Connecticut at the time, I was going through a seven-mile long stretch of a construction zone. Cops galore. I have long hair and casually hid my phone in my hair to hear that Killian must have eaten his entire internal padding for his bed because Dr. Dutton pulled and pulled and pulled and pulled and pulled enough stuffing to make the blizzard of '78 look like a mere dusting. We discussed post operative care, what to look for in terms of complications, bland diet protocol, and within a week, Killian should be well on to the road to recovery.

I got back home from the meeting later than I wanted. I was able to pick up Killian though and he was the picture of misery. He was hunched in pain, moving very slowly, and had such an empty look in his eyes. I brought Killian home and saw my in laws for a brief moment before they were off to go to Jason's mother's house for the evening. I set up Killian's bed in the living room since stairs would be too difficult for him and his incision could become compromised by such activity. I also brought my blankets downstairs so I could sleep next to him.

The following 4 days, I never left Killian's side. For the first 36 hours, the poor dog endured his temperature taken every hour, incision checks, constant checking to make sure his gums were pink and moist and various other vital sign checks. Being that it was a holiday weekend, Dr. Dutton told me I could call him at home. The emergency clinic was being very patient with me as I was calling at the slightest anything, which included a temperature reading that was 0.3 degrees higher than normal. That Sunday, in a round about way, Jason asked if I wanted a break and wanted to go to his family's Christmas party. For a brief moment, the scene in the movie Top Gun flashed through my mind, and there was no hesitation when I said, "I'm not leaving my wingman." Dave and Vicki took pity on me and brought home a full spread dinner of steak and vegetables, champagne and other goodies. I propped up Killian on a bed in the breakfast nook and we shot pool and had a nice evening and I was distracted from my nurse duties of my dog for a few hours.

Killian made a full recovery and has since lost the hope of ever having a bed in his crate. Every once in a while I feel bad and try to give him at the very least a blanket which he inevitably eats. Recently, I accidentally left him uncrated during the day. He ripped down the window grate on the sliding glass door that leads to the deck. I can only imagine his terror as the whole thing, which is about five feet tall, came crashing down on him. He also managed to chew the door handle on the front door as an attempt to escape.

When we built our house it was with the hopes of it staying nice. When you add a dog to anything "nice," that hope just goes right out the window.

# Aurora's Homecoming

When Jason and I first married, we bought a cute little 858 square foot condominium. It was perfect for a couple starting out on their own, or even as a retirement home. The landscaping was beautiful. There were people who plowed and shoveled the snow in the winter. There was a pool and tennis courts. The vacuum cord easily went from one end of the house to the other for easy cleaning. We lived on the top floor and had a great view of the treetops from our windows.

Our commutes were greatly reduced from where we had been living before. I went from a 35-mile commute on back roads to a 6-mile commute, most of which was highway. Jason went from a 45-mile commute, which was all back roads, and one irritatingly long drive down a road that brings new meaning to the word commercialism. There is a shopping plaza every 15 feet with a minimum of 15 stores per plaza. If you hit one red light on that road, you will hit every subsequent red light at each of the shopping plazas and it will indeed tack on 20 minutes to your commute. His new commute was now fewer than 30 minutes, all highway driving. We had delivery of pizza, Chinese food; the grocery store was .6 mile down the road. The mortgage was under $500, including taxes. We were in heaven.

Then, about four years later, the itch set in. We renovated the condo until we couldn't renovate it any more. We had put in tile flooring. We added a heating element in the bathroom so the floor was now heated and we had toasty toes upon exiting the shower. We put a new vanity and toilet in the bathroom. We put in new counters in the kitchen. We painted every room so the house was filled with warmth and color. Suddenly, 858 square feet was getting awfully small. Our storage units were filled to maximum capacity with all the stuff we couldn't get rid of, but wouldn't fit in the condo itself. The housing market was a sellers' dream. We found a piece of 5-acre property for an absolute steal. Since I had changed jobs, the property was now 5 miles from my new job. We were going to live the dream of building our own home just the way we wanted it.

That dream became a nightmare, and to this day, I will look back and say it sucked and I will never do it again. However, now my house is beautiful and I am grateful to everyone who helped us persevere through it. My mom was especially supportive. I would send repeated text messages that I hated my life and instead of the usual "Suck it up" response I was used to getting, she was very understanding that building a house is stressful and she would reply, "I know." For her, that's pretty darn supportive.

Once the house was completed to the inspector and banks' standards, it was time to get another dog. Some people will say "new house new baby." That so wasn't going to happen in my case. I am not Mom material. I'm a dog person through and through. In fact, I'm the reason I chose not to have kids. I was an awful child and do not question why I was sent to boarding school.

I digress. At that point, we only had Killian. Again, Killian is indeed my favorite and I will willingly sell my soul for that dog, but in terms of home or personal protection, I'm not his wingman. If Bad Man breaks into our house and wants to kill me, Killian will be showing him where the cheese is and can he please have some when Bad Man is done dismembering me.

I had fallen in love with the Bullmastiff breed and decided that would be our next dog. Oddly enough, it was a Bullmastiff that was being put to sleep for biting a child that sparked my interest. The dog had been peacefully sleeping and the child had jumped on the dog, startling her. She reacted by biting the child in the face and he did require several stitches. It was a horribly sad situation because the child made the mistake of waking a sleeping dog, and the dog made the mistake of reacting like she did.

Before she could be put to sleep, the owners had to abide by New Hampshire state law and quarantine the dog for ten days. They boarded her during those ten days at the animal hospital. Every day, I would go in early and bring her cheese, or chicken, or just extra yummies, and I would just sit with her and tell her she was a good girl and I loved her. The day she died was a horribly painful one, for everyone. I was unable to assist the doctor even though her owner had asked for me because I was in the back of the hospital unable to hold back the tears.

I took it as my mission to be an advocate for this powerful yet truly gentle breed. I researched the breed on line. I bought books regarding the temperament and was continually impressed at the loyalty and level of owner protection the dog provides. That was the dog I wanted. I saw too many horror movies when I was too young and am now thoroughly afraid of the dark. Jason travels a great deal for his job. We live in the woods. My closest neighbor is 100 yards away. If I'm in trouble, no one will hear my scream. I wanted a dog that was 100-pound coach potato but whose presence alone was enough to make anyone think twice.

I went through the American Bullmastiff Association and filled out an adoption application. Within a few weeks, the Vermont

ABA Rescue Coordinator, Colleen, contacted me. She had an intact female who was found wandering in a state park in Massachusetts. After spending ten days in the local pound waiting for her owners to come claim her, no one did, Aurora was turned over to Bullmastiff Rescue.

It was a grueling two weeks convincing Colleen we would make a good home for Aurora. However, now that I too am a volunteer for ABA, the two of us are a force to be reckoned with. We want holiday cards and updates, but we never want to see our foster dogs in a rescue situation again, so we are very thorough to say the least about our screening process. That being said, this was my first time on the receiving end of Colleen's intensity and it was draining. I couldn't understand what the hold up was. I was a vet tech for crying out loud, I was going to feed Science Diet, and I had the Invisible Fence® for containment to keep the dog in my yard. What was the problem?

Her answers were simple: no matter what your job title is, you can still run the potential to be a moron who shouldn't own a cactus. I didn't fit in that category but she needed to be sure. Colleen preferred a higher quality food that didn't have corn or by products as primary ingredients. Lastly, there is a very strict policy on Invisible Fence® containment that required professional lessons as well as installation of the fence and even then ABA doesn't welcome the Invisible Fence® with open arms due to owner error concerns.

Eventually, we were able to come to agreements on her concerns and the adoption was approved. Being that I was still working for Dr. Dutton, he gave a very generous discount to his staff members and my cost was cheaper than Colleen's cost for spaying a dog, I agreed to spay the dog. The contract stated I had to do it within 72 hours of the adoption and then I had to fax the spay certificate to the Director of ABA Rescue as well as Colleen. Believe me when I say that clock was ticking, and there wasn't a snooze button.

By Bullmastiff breed standards, Aurora is a large female. She isn't fat by any means, but she is a big boned, solid, tall, and powerful girl with a very large head. She had clearly had at least one litter of puppies, as her mammary chain was very pronounced. I promptly bought her a Hooters shirt because, well, I am *that* dog owner. We dubbed her Big Mama after she charged the television during an episode of Animal Cops that had a litter of puppies crying and she was very concerned.

Aurora had clearly come from a loving and lenient home. Too lenient I think. There is a family that isn't missing a dog; they are missing their *Princess*. She walked into our house and immediately got up on the couch with a look of, "I belong up here. A dog of my stature does not lie on *the floor.*" When I made her dinner of dog kibble, she looked at my plate of chicken like I was clearly mistaken in who should eat what. A dog of her stature doesn't eat *dog food*. My mistake. Not. Eat your dog food or start chipping in for your food, that's the motto at our house.

When it was time for bed, we went upstairs to the bedroom. She walked in, surveyed the situation, and jumped right up on our bed and proceeded to hog it all night long. We were novices at the time and thought it would be nice for her to sleep with us. That honeymoon was short to say the least as I very much set myself up to fail by allowing such freedom so early on in the relationship. The next night, it was just the dogs and I. Jason was out of town and again, I let her on the bed because I wanted something between me and the door should Bad Man break into the house. To this day, she still is allowed, via invitation only, on the bed when Jason is out of town, but we have a much better understanding of who runs the show… It's not her.

The next morning, Aurora felt it was time to get up. She got off the bed and started her low growl to say it was time to get up. I told her to go lie down; it wasn't time to get up yet.

She continued her growl and this time ended it with a bark as if to tell me, "No really. Get up. I'm serious."

To which I replied, "No really. Go lie down. I'm serious too." I loved my new girl but it was going to be a cold day in Hades before I let a dog tell me when it's time to get up. She proceeded to slam into the bed with her massive head until she knocked it off the frame. I got up.

Score 1 point for the dog.

# AND PORTER MAKES FOUR

Denali was a special dog. They are all special, but Denali had a certain quality that made him unique. Was he unique because he was no longer loved by his previous owner and surrendered to Dogue de Bordeaux Rescue Society? No. Was he exceptional because someone abused him with a broom? Not necessarily. Was he different because he had developed aggression issues with men due to his sad past? Not even a little bit. What made him different was once he was given a constant source of love; he defended that supply with ferocity and devotion unparalleled to any dog I have ever met. Denali's motto was, "defend Mom and bite first, ask questions later." I have never felt safer than when he was at my side.

Am I proud I had an aggressive dog? No. I make no excuses for aggression. However, I did not make him the defendant he was. Poor treatment did that. I did my best to curb the aggression and give him the appropriate tools at redirection and obedience. Bordeauxs tend to bond with one owner over another. Denali was very much *my* dog. In fact, for the first year he was with us, he *barely* tolerated Jason. There was one night I had gone out with friends leaving the dogs with Jason for the evening. I came home to discover it had been a hard night for everyone. Denali wouldn't let Jason near him. He kept the pool table between him and Jason the whole evening barking at Jason to stay away. When I came home, I sat on the floor with Denali, and when Jason came to sit with us, Denali curled his lip at Jason. Over the months, Jason wormed his way into Denali's heart, but Denali's loyalty was with me.

Jason did his best to have Dad and Denali time though. Dump Day was always a special day for them. Every Saturday, one of Jason's chores is to take the trash to the transfer station. Every Saturday, Jason would reach for his redneck, flannel jacket. God, I hate that thing. As soon as Denali saw the "John boy" jacket in Jason's hand, his big floppy paws would start going everywhere. He actually smiled a big toothy grin. This was their exclusive time. Jason would open the window of his truck and Denali, regardless of the temperature, had his head out the window, his loose lips flopping in the wind, all but changing the trajectory of the truck. When they got home, Denali would find me and hop all around me, bouncing with happiness about his latest adventure.

Denali went through phases where he wasn't aggressive or even snappy. He was a favorite in many circles because when he was good, he was *great*. He was a sweet boy with a happy disposition. But, for whatever reason, he would have these little set backs that would turn our little bundle of fur into a deadly force of fury.

Four months prior to his death, Denali's aggression hit a new level of danger. No one, especially a man, was able to be within fifty feet of me without Denali lunging, barking, and snarling. In March, we were on a walk on the trail behind our house with all four of the dogs. I had Denali and Killian on their leashes; Jason had Aurora and Tatum on their leashes. We rounded the corner and another couple with their beagle was walking toward us. Denali went bezerk and I had to make the choice of letting go of Killian because I needed two hands to restrain the 120 pounds of muscle that was now, as Cesar Millan puts it, "in the red zone." Someone could get hurt or killed when Denali loses his composure.

It was also evident he wasn't feeling well. He seemed mopey, not on his game, and just not right. In April, it was just the two of us on a walk in the neighborhood by our house. About a third of the way into the walk, his tongue went blue and his gums were white. That's *never* a good sign. I got him home as quickly as I could and immediately called Dr. Dutton. He recommended doing another ultrasound of his heart to see how his Pulmonary Stenosis was progressing. Dr. Zimmerman recommended Dr. John MacGregor at the Dover Animal Hospital. He was a Board Certified Cardiologist. It all made sense, if he was sick, of course he was grumpy. Let's get him feeling better and life would be cheery again.

While in the waiting room at the Dover Animal Hospital, the UPS delivery person walked through the door. Denali charged him. I had a firm grip on the leash so Denali only made it four feet in his charge at defending me from the evil man in brown who was clearly going to box me up and ship me into the unknown. My energy was shot at that point. Dear God, Dr. MacGregor needed to fix my loose cannon of a dog before someone got killed.

Dr. MacGregor is a warm, sensitive, matter of fact doctor who was nothing short of wonderful but he does not sugar coat poop when discussing diagnoses. His staff and attending technicians were also supportive and very compassionate. In terms of his coronary condition, Denali didn't have Pulmonary Stenosis as we were originally told; Dr. MacGregor found Doodles had Subaortic Stenosis. My dog has been on the wrong medication for over two years and oh by the way, his Stenosis wasn't really *that* bad that it would be causing the aggression. Sure, he may have days when he felt awful and the heat never did him any favors, but his heart wasn't the source of the aggression.

When I got home, I mulled over the cardiac report as well as the original diagnostic report from the Board Certified Internist who originally did Snoodle's ultrasound. Wait a minute, I thought, they are both Board Certified. Hmmmmm. Who do I believe? I called Dr. Dutton. He placed a call to both doctors and since the original doctor never did a Doppler test (I have no idea what that means but apparently, it's pretty important), according to Dr. MacGregor, and Dr. Dutton agreed, without the confirming Doppler test, "there is no way in hell Denali has Pulmonary Stenosis." That solves that issue.

I called my friend who still uses that veterinary clinic occasionally and I was spewing pure poison. And to be honest, it wasn't that this doctor misdiagnosed my dog. Well, maybe it was a little, but at the time, Denali had been in the care of the rescue group. A group with limited financial resources. That diagnosis was not only incorrect, but also expensive! Know your stuff before you sentence a dog to death, since essentially, the Ultrasound report recommended euthanizing him and not waste rescue resources on a lost cause. My angel was *not* a lost cause.

Now we have a new diagnosis and the *appropriate* medication but that still leaves the aggression issues. Again, I relied on the expertise of Carol and Art Landry and we put Denali in a Level II obedience class. He passed with flying colors and it really seemed to give him the tools to understand that not every situation required his teeth. It was funny to watch Denali. The class was an hour long and it was a five week class. Every week, you could set your watch to the minute when Denali would check out of the lesson. The class started at 7:00. At 7:42, Denali would lie down and unless we were leaving, he wasn't getting up. In fact, during some of the Sit/Down Stay exercises, I would have to tell him to "Sit. Stay. Stay awake!" That should have been a clue, but we just figured he was tired and bored with doing stuff he already knew how to do. There were even a couple of other dogs that also had aggression issues in the class and a few teeth flashed from time to time, but on the whole, Denali did awesome and I beamed with pride at our special little dog. I truly feel a structured obedience class is crucial for not only owner/dog communication, but also dog-to-dog communication skills are also developed.

At the end of the six week class, Denali wasn't feeling any better. Three doctors, Dr. Dutton, Dr. Zimmerman, and Dr. Ham all found different areas to elicit pain in his back but no one could tell us why and the next step was to consider was the neurology aspect. While I couldn't afford an MRI or CAT scan, we could at least do a neurological consult. We went to a neurologist because x rays, blood work, and a chiropractor all found different sore spots in Denali's spine, and now he was crying in pain when going up and down stairs. This was a dog that would take a bullet for me; the least I could do is empty my bank account to fix him.

By all accounts, I'm nothing if not thorough. Before his appointment, I made sure I forwarded a copy of Denali's chart to the neurologist who was in Maine. In just over two years, D's medical chart was over 80 pages. My whole point of forwarding it was to make sure *before* we stepped through the door, the doctor had a complete history and I didn't need to spend the appointment answering questions that were already explained in the chart.

The appointment was at 8:00 AM in Portland. I left the house at 5:45 to make sure traffic wouldn't be a factor. Normally, it's about an hour and a half drive from our house. Since I left before any real rush hour traffic commenced, I got there at 7:15. I found a Dunkin Donuts and had another coffee. Denali had a few munchkins and went back to sleep in the back of my truck.

At 7:55, Denali and I went into the clinic and were ushered into the exam room. Imagine my irritation when it was 8:07 when the doctor and technician strolled into the appointment. One of the many lessons I learned while in the employ of Dr. Dutton was 1. Don't keep the client waiting 2. If the client is early, see her early so you don't get held up by any complications 3. The sooner you complete your appointments, the sooner you can go home. This doctor didn't subscribe to those practices. She takes a brief history of Denali which included several questions that were noted previously in his chart, she does a very thorough exam, then excuses herself and her assistant to go read Denali's chart.

I could hear them discussing the chart as she was clearly reading it for the first time and I was in the exam room *seething* with irritation. The idea of seeing a neurologist wasn't because I was unhappy with my regular veterinarians; it was because my dog needed a specialist. I would assume no two cases are identical so really, do your homework before the exam. I'm just saying. This appointment was my last hope for Denali. Dr. Dutton didn't have any more magic rabbits in his hat. Dr. Zimmerman couldn't put on her red boots and cape and be Super Doctor. If the neurology appointment didn't pan out, it was time to accept the already setting sun on our dog and do what was best for Denali so when I didn't feel the doctor was truly prepared for what was facing her, the life and death of my boy, I was livid.

After lots of whispering in the hall, the doctor comes back in and says she thinks Denali has Endocarditis. In my head, I'm going through the various syllables and their medical meaning (again thank you Dr. Dutton) "Endo" means within. "Card" refers to the heart. "Itis" is an infection. OK, so he has an infection within the heart. That's what is making my dog scream in pain when he goes up and down stairs? It seemed a little far-fetched but I don't have initials after my name, what do I know? She excuses herself to prepare a prescription.

While I was waiting for her to return with the medication, I immediately fired off an e mail to Dr. Dutton, Dr. Zimmerman, and Dr. Ham to get their take on the diagnosis. I have to say this; they all displayed a commendable level of professionalism with their surprise at that diagnosis. Jason and Dr. Dutton were one step ahead of me and called Dr. MacGregor. I believe Dr. MacGregor's response was "There was NO WAY Denali had Endocarditis. Not even on a lukewarm day in hell." The diagnosis is so unbelievably rare that while it is possible *my* dog has it only because he is *my* dog, even in this case, it was pretty unlikely.

Short of doing a CAT scan or an MRI which may or may not prove a diagnosis, it would have required sedation and I wasn't sure Denali could withstand it in his weakened condition. We also weren't guaranteed the ability to fix anything due to his heart condition because most likely he would have needed surgery. We opted to put Denali to sleep. Dr. Dutton came to our house. Under the Oak trees in our front yard, our precious dog, my beloved protector was gone. As he was passing away, he let out a little snore to let us know he was finally at peace.

I know what happens to a pet when they die in terms of what happens to their remains. They are lovingly placed in a plastic cadaver bag and gingerly positioned in a freezer until the pet cemetery people come and carefully set the frozen remains of the pet into the back of the truck until it reaches the cemetery or crematorium. I was absolutely sick at the thought of Doodles shoved into a trash bag, or crammed in a freezer, and then being hurled into the bed of a truck like a piece of garbage. We elected to have a private cremation where *we* brought his remains to the crematorium and *we* waited while he was incinerated and *we* immediately got his ashes back. As an aside, don't watch them put your pet into the cremation oven. Just don't. The last memory you should have of your pet should not be of your beloved going into an oven.

The people at the crematorium were beyond the definition of wonderful. Everyone from the receptionist at the desk who was warm and caring to the boys who lovingly placed Denali into a casket surrounded by flowers and candles was wonderful. Mike, one of the attendants of the pets, was especially compassionate. He has an ability to read owners' pain and performs his job with such sensitivity that he deserves special recognition.

It takes a very strong person to do that job. I need to be able to laugh every day, even if it's at myself, which it usually is. But to see people every day aching over the loss of their beloved furry friend, and that day I was inconsolable, working on the other side of that counter would bring about a depression that requires horse sedatives for me. The receptionist handed me a poem, "I'm Still Here" and oh my Christmas, I just put my head on the counter and sobbed. My angel was gone. I would never hug him again, and yet here is a poem stating he is still watching over me. I cried until I passed out as we drove home that afternoon.

The following few months were a combination of sadness, rage, and acceptance, often in a matter of moments. The Fray's song How to Save a Life reduced me to tears in a nanosecond. And it seemed the episode of Scrubs when Ben died played quite a bit in the repeat rotation on Comedy Central and it continued to remind me how I failed Denali.

Gradually, the deafening silence of not having Denali was overbearing. The emptiness in the house that lacked the powerful presence of a Bordeaux started hurting as much as the loss of Denali itself. Not to mention I had to drive by the tree sign in our driveway every day that read "Dogue de Bordeaux Crossing" and it was killing me. I started filling my time researching Bordeaux breeders. There is just nothing cuter on this planet than a Bordeaux puppy. Yeah, they grow up to be wrinkley and in the minds of some, goofy looking. But those big round eyes, squishy faces, and soulful expressions just melt your heart when they are babies.

I had contacted a few breeders with a lengthy description of the lifestyle we lead, the devotion to our dogs we have, and I attached many pictures depicting what life as our dog looks like. I spoke with breeders in Texas, Michigan, and New Jersey. The phone rang one day. It was the Director of Dogue de Bordeaux Rescue in Oregon. There were two six month old puppies in Pennsylvania who had been surrendered to rescue and she wanted the puppies to go to people who are within the realms of rescue. The female had been spoken for but the male was still available. Were we interested? I looked at Jason and his eyes just lit up with happiness. He missed his big boy as much as I did. And since this guy was still a puppy, there was a hope in hell this dog would like him, love him even. We agreed. We would meet his foster mom in three weeks in Pennsylvania.

Two days before we were set to road trip I was in a car accident. Anyone who knows me has called me Crash at least once. I don't exactly have the best driving record. The first time Jason and I "officially" dated, I wrapped his car around a tree within 2 weeks into the relationship. The first car my Dad bought me, I backed into a brick wall and then four months later slammed it into a guardrail during a snowstorm. Oh, and I've rear ended a few cars too. Well, two cars and one 18 wheeler. However, *this* particular accident wasn't my fault.

It was a glorious August day. Sunny. Hot, but not oppressive or humid. My schedule was busy but not slamming busy. There was a lot of driving but the girl at Dunkin Donuts made my coffee just right. I was making my way to my final call singly loudly and off key I'm sure. I was behind an SUV that was towing a trailer with two four wheelers on it and a spare tire.

The spare tire wasn't secured properly to the trailer. They must have hit a bump because all of a sudden the tire popped off the trailer and was rolling down the road at me. I was following at a safe distance, and I still haven't done the math to determine the rate of speed the tire was coming at me, but the bottom line was I didn't have time to react. The tire went under the front of my car and launched that little Prius like the General Lee in Dukes of Hazard.

Thankfully, there wasn't any on coming traffic because I bounced in the middle of the road like a kangaroo upon landing before I could pull over. The people in the SUV didn't stop, but they also didn't know anything had happened. A man in a vehicle behind me saw it and stopped to see if I was okay, which I was, shaken up, but okay. My car was all messed up. We were in No Signal Ville so calling into work was difficult. A police officer drove by and stopped. Then the people whose tire was now in the ditch also came back.

We exchanged the appropriate information. The officer took a "statement" and I limped my little puppy car to the gas station down the street so I could call the office. I still didn't have consistent cell signal so I was using the pay phone, talking to the manager on duty in the office at work, taking pictures of the damage with my cell phone to prove a Prius can't fly. I felt confident I could get my car to the garage for repairs when my back started hurting.

By the time I made it to the garage, I was in significant discomfort. Jason picked me up at the garage and standing upright was now an issue for me. Well, since this accident wasn't my fault and had someone else's insurance to pick up the tab, off to the ER I went. X rays were clear and I was sent home with some amazing painkillers. Holy cow! I took one Friday night and I don't think I woke up til Sunday. These are rainy day drugs.

Sunday morning at 4:00, Jason poured me into the Jimmy and we made the trek to Pennsylvania to get our new little Bordeaux. I think I woke up somewhere outside of Hartford. We were bubbling with excitement. Dogue de Bordeauxs are like potato chips. You can't have just one. We couldn't wait to get there.

A few hours later, we were on our way home with our new little boy. He barely had any fur due to his mange. But his eyes melted your soul. He just had this expression that asked, "Will you love me? I wasn't loved enough." We stopped off at my mother's house on the way home and he had his first bully stick.

Whereas Denali was very much *my* dog, we tried to encourage a deeper bond with Jason and Porter. Yeah right. It was at best a cute attempt. Initially, Jason was the one who held the leash on walks. Jason fed Porter. Jason was even the one who chose the name Porter because in old French times, the Porter was the Doorkeeper and what an appropriate role for a Dogue de Bordeaux. Jason could have sat on a couch made of cheese with Porter and Porter would still be my dog. One night, it was solidified in no uncertain terms.

Tatum is resource aggressive when it comes to other dogs and objects or people she deems as hers. A person can take her food from her while it's in her mouth and she'll relinquish it without question. She will look at you like this is the worst game ever but she won't protest in any way but a pout. However, if a dog tries to take a bone she is chewing, or really within a mile of her, fur will fly. Tatum was chewing on a bone and Porter thought it was his turn for the bone. I was making dinner for the dogs when all of a sudden I hear snarling. I looked over and saw Porter jumping back from Tatum's fangs and in doing so, knocked over the bar stool that went crashing onto the tile. Porter was screaming in fear and probably pain since his muzzle now had a few holes. I caught Porter as he was fleeing in terror, wrapped all around him and held him with his arm buried in my chest until he stopped crying, which took about 5 minutes. As a rule, dogs don't cry unless they are in pain, but Porter's voice had the tone of fear and it was heart wrenching to hear him so upset. In that instant, he became *my* dog but what was I going to do? Not comfort him? Riiiiight. And don't get me wrong, I do not coddle drama, but this incident was beyond a little scuffle and Porter needed reassurance he wasn't brought into this house to be Tatum's chew toy. Well, not before he could at least fend for himself.

At that point, I had to make the choice to not *kill* Tatum or even yell at her since the moment had passed and she wouldn't know why I was a raving lunatic, but believe me when I say I was raging. When Porter was calm, we went into the kitchen so I could see that damage the Imp inflicted. He had a few bite wounds and I started putting lavender on the cuts but it was nothing serious so there wasn't a mad dash to the vet's office. There were blood spots all over my sweatshirt when Jason walked in the door. He came over and saw what I was doing and asked what happened. I icily informed him Tatum was now *his* dog and she is very lucky I haven't tied her to a tree at the end of our driveway with a sign that reads "Free to A Home. Good Optional."

A few days later, Porter was no worse for the wear and starting to play with Tatum. She taught him all her moves. The body check. The chest slam. The play bow then pounce. Tatum and Porter, with his gigantic paws, were bombing around the house and yard like long lost pals. A couple days later, Porter had his vaccines and it was time to send him to daycare to learn appropriate dog social tools.

Our house felt complete again. Porter made four.

# MANGY MUTT

Porter was 7 months old when we adopted him. His story is a sad one. While his isn't a story of abuse, neglect, and terror, it is a story of lack of love, just when he needed it most. He and his sister came from Hungary. At 8 weeks of age, they were sold to a broker in Pennsylvania who placed them in separate pet stores.

Dogs go through what is called "Imprint phases." These Imprint Phases are crucial in determining who the dog will become. For example, a thunderstorm for a dog during an Imprint Phase can be a scary thing and create a dog that had never before shown fear of storms into a dog that will now shred a garage to pieces even when under heavy sedation like John Grogan's beloved Marley. Porter simply wasn't loved enough as a puppy, or even at all for that matter when he desperately needed to be shown human kindness. It was during that infant Imprint Phase when he never developed the human-dog bond; Porter developed his wariness of strangers, namely men.

He and his sister, Delilah, both had Demodex Mange and Porter had developed a horrible infection that affected his lymph nodes. Neither dog made it to the pet store floor. Neither dog was ever put up for sale due to their poor health. One lymph node on Porter was the size of a baseball when the manager of the store called Dogue de Bordeaux rescue and said the store would not be able to sell the dogs and would rescue take them into its program. Bordeaux Rescue took the dogs and we adopted little Porter.

After several months of unsuccessfully treating Porter's mange with oral Ivermectin, Dr. Dutton finally had a Come to Jesus talk with me. He had been trying to get me to do a Mitaban dip since August. I had been protesting tooth and nail. Mitaban is a highly toxic pesticide and while hundreds of dogs get dipped every year and live to bark about it, it is not without risk. I was trying to avoid those risks by trying the most au naturelle route as possible. It wasn't working.

To apply Mitaban, a 10 ml bottle needs to be diluted in two *gallons* of water. You need to be wearing gloves to touch the mixture and be in a well-ventilated area. Now you want me to put that on my dog? I was happy to keep trying the Ivermectin but Dr. Dutton urged me to reconsider. The dog was still 40% bald. He stunk horribly of yeast and just plain ick. His skin was starting to crack and callous. For a dog of his age and stature, Porter was still quite small for his breed, barely breaking 70 pounds. In all honesty, the mange was really taxing his immune system by the continual fight it was enduring trying to cure the mange. In some cases, mange can be fatal. Dr. Dutton again assured me my precious pooch would be fine, better even. I relented. I set up the appointment for the dip.

As usual, whenever I made a decision about the dogs, or really anything short of wardrobe questions, I called Maureen to make sure I wasn't going to kill my dog. She agreed that while we try to follow the natural homeopathic route of the Eastern world, Western medicine also has its advantages and sometimes, we have to cross over and let the chemicals do their job.

I opted to let the technicians at the Weare Animal Hospital do the dip. The first and painfully obvious reason is I didn't want to do it was because I would screw it up. One 10 ml bottle cost $27.00 and I didn't want to be the idiot to spill it. Second, he was going to need a series of these dips and I didn't want him to see me walk into the bathroom and then anticipate what was coming next which would entail me chasing him all over the house. Third, performing these dips is a pain in the neck. The dog needs a regular bath with special Benzoyle Peroxide shampoo. After he is dry from that bath, you then pour the Mitaban dip mixture on the dog and he has to drip dry. The process takes about four hours. Yeah, I'll pass on that and let the professionals do their thing.

Jason picked up Porter after his bath. Porter didn't seem any worse for the wear, and life was good. The stench of chemical was in the air that evening. Before he smelled of mangy mutt. Now he reeked of the Dow Chemical plant. My nostrils were on fire and eyes were watering it was so powerful. Personally, I preferred the aroma of mangy mutt.

Side effect of Mitaban Number One: According to the Pfizer website: "Transient sedation may occur after treatment with this product." My dog was stoned out of his gourd. He ate his dinner and plopped on his bed and was out for the night. I actually felt bad waking him for his late night potty walk. I should have counted my blessings he was sleeping.

The days following the dip were pure misery. The following morning, he was still out of sorts and needy, and even for Porter, he was exceptionally clingy. If I wasn't physically touching him, he would poke me with his nose until he got his head rubbed with his big huge eyes and an expression that ached for attention. I had the day off and was in bed playing on the computer surfing the latest and greatest orthopedic dog bed or something shiny for the dogs. I don't always practice what I preach about obedience and coddling drama and I don't care sometimes. This was my boy and he needed Mom love. He was all but trembling on the side of the bed begging to come up. I don't care that I was coddling and reassuring pathetic behaviors; he didn't feel well and I wrapped him in a fleece blanket and let him snuggle with me on Jason's pillow. He was asleep in minutes.

That afternoon and evening, he was a mess. He was so itchy and uncomfortable he shredded himself open with his nails. He had sores from his scratching from his head all the way down his sides ending at his tail where he had chewed that raw too. He was pacing from the living room to the dog room. He would lie in Aurora's crate. Ten seconds later he would go to the living room to his elephant bed and lie down on that for a minute in the hopes of finding somewhere to be comfortable. Then repeat this about 100 more times. I was pumping him with Benadryl, spraying the sores with lavender, and quietly having a meltdown. I called the vet and was told to put socks on him and his lampshade collar. He was up the entire night scratching and chewing. This meant I was up the entire night trying to stop him from scratching and chewing. At one point, I slept on the floor with him to try to soothe him. Jason slept through the whole thing.

The following day the doctor prescribed a round of antibiotics. It was an absolute blizzard that day and I had been called off the roads for work. Not to be undaunted by unplowed roads, my little pup needed me. I hopped in my big girl truck and away I went to get the medication. I bought more lavender for his wounds and kept pumping him full of Benadryl. He seemed a little better in terms of cognizance, but still itchy as can be and he looked like he had road rash from his sores. The next day, since he was still miserable, I picked up some sedatives from the animal hospital and I was liberal with the dosage. Again, I went above and beyond the coddling of our little man but we both needed sleep at that point. When the dogs don't sleep, I don't sleep. I decided he could sleep in bed with us. He spent all night snuggled with me, snoring in my face and farting in Jason's.

We did a total of four more Mitaban dips over the course of three months. While he never had the itchy reaction of scratching himself to a bloody pulp like he did with the first dip, he would come home reeking of chemicals and was intensely needy and out of sorts the following two days. But he was getting fur and didn't smell bad anymore.

As time went on and his coat grew, we discovered he has some white fur on his toes and little feather tufts on his legs. With his fur, Porter is a stunning Dogue de Bordeaux. He has a gorgeous head and remarkable coloring. He also started to actually grow once his immune system could relax. He gained twenty pounds in three months and was finally filling out and looking like a true Dogue de Bordeaux. At his final recheck appointment at the vet, Porter was deemed cured. Dr. Dutton walked into the exam room pumping his fists chanting, "Go Western Medicine. Go Western Medicine. Go Western Medicine." Smartass.

# A Tale Of Two Testicles

As part of the adoption agreement for Porter, I agreed to neuter Porter when his mange was cured. Prior to the Mitaban dip, he had a negative skin scraping when he was 10 months old and I was cleared to neuter him. As a woman and unlike most men when it comes to talking about Man Land, I have no qualms whatsoever about neutering a male, canine or otherwise. In fact, the very last thing I want in my house is an intact dog, male or female. Porter was coming into sexual maturity and really becoming a pushy little boy. It was time to snip those suckers off.

As it turned out, even though the skin scraping itself was negative, he would still suffer from the side effects of the mange. In fact, he had a relapse shortly after that negative scraping and those little bugs kept chewing his fur til he was bald again and caused complications during his neuter. Porter had a horrible time clotting his blood during the surgery. Dr. Dutton had e mailed me after the surgery to let me know of the situation and gave me options. I could do warm compresses on his incision and do a ten day course of antibiotics. Or, I could have the doctor to go back in to Porter's scrotal sac, remove the giant blood clot and cauterize the blood cells. Lastly, I could run various screenings to check for blood clotting disorders, including Von Willibrands disease. Being that Plan B sounded awfully painful, and expensive, I opted for the warm compresses. I would run the blood work later.

When I picked him up that afternoon, he was the picture of pure pathetic. His back was hunched, he was swaggering and unbalanced, his eyes droopy, and just a big bundle of "Poor Me." Audra, one of the attending technicians, had told me just how pitiful the little boy had been. As he was emerging into the world of consciousness after the surgery and the anesthesia was wearing off, Audra asked Porter how he was feeling. He didn't open an eye, wag his tail, or even perk his ears. He was lying on his side and he lifted one leg to show her that something was clearly missing and he would like them back.

He did start licking at his incision during his recovery from anesthesia and he would need to be restrained from getting at the incision while he recovered for the next seven to ten days. I loathe the Elizabethan lampshade collars so I elected for a Bite Not® collar. Those collars look like the neck braces one wears after an accident or injury and has to maintain neck immobility. It allows the dog to see, eat, drink, and walk while at the same time limiting neck movement and often creates enough of a strain it is not worth the dogs' efforts to get around the collar. Most dogs do fine with this sort of collar, but my dogs are not most dogs.

Within five days, it was very apparent Porter could strain his neck far enough to get to his incision, and he started licking it open. I reluctantly agreed he needed to wear the lampshade collar. Since his incision was now somewhat open, little drips of blood were now all over my house. Sometimes, when he would do a nose to toes shake after a good stretch, he would shake spit and blood everywhere, including the ceiling. If the CSI unit ever needs to come to my house, that could create some awkward moments. It was just such fun times.

But it gets better. I went back to the Animal Hospital and they sent me home with a 25-inch wide collar. As it turned out, 25 inches was just what Porter needed to use the edge of his collar completely rip open his incision. Blood was everywhere. He was hunched in pain again and now there were chunks in his blood.

It was Sunday morning and we were now at the end of his second week of his recovery. After a pool of blood formed while he sat and watched me in the bathroom brush my teeth. Jason came in to the bathroom, saw the puddle of blood and how arced Porter's back was and he said Porter needed medical attention, now. Jason usually subscribes to the wait and see school of thought, especially since it was $85 just to walk through the door of the Veterinary Emergency Clinic with our pup. Even I was going to keep an eye on it and call Dr. Dutton in the morning. However, if he feels our boy needs medical attention, well then away we go. I called the Emergency Room and they told us to come down.

My hope was that they would anesthetize him and resuture his incision. It wasn't to be. They did run a clotting screening, which was normal. The concern was he might have an infection inside his testicles and with an open wound; it is best to let the infection heal from the inside out but to not enclose that infection. That just gives everyone the warm fuzzies, doesn't it? We were sent home with more antibiotics and a 30-inch lampshade. When he would walk the whole lampshade would bob up and down a good five inches. He was indeed the goofiest sight you ever saw.

At this point, I really started doing the warm compresses in earnest and my dog would see those compresses and assume the position like a seasoned prostitute, on his back with his legs in the air. The first time I applied the compress I had Jason help me. He held Porter's head while I applied the cloth. At first, Porter was confused and resisted with an, "I beg your pardon. What do you think…? Hey, wait a minute… Aaaaaaahhhhhhhhhh. That feels really good."

One afternoon, my day at work was light and I was set free from the time clock to go do as I pleased. Oh, such opportunities. It was a gorgeous day. I could walk the other dogs. Run errands. Do the mountain of laundry that was accumulating. Fold the other mountain of laundry that had accumulated. I could scoop poop in the yard. Get dinner started. Well, OK *that* wasn't going to happen since cooking isn't my forte. Instead, I spent my afternoon of freedom holding a warm washcloth to my dog's hind end. There are days it is just painful how badly I need a second hobby.

# Miss Cleo

Bullmastiffs have a predisposition of developing hypothyroidism. Just like with people, it truly isn't that big deal once the thyroid is regulated. The medication is lifelong but not expensive. When Aurora was 6, I was having a bear of a time getting weight off her. She was almost 140 pounds where her ideal weight should have been 120 pounds. She looked like a whiskey barrel and I was getting very offended and very defensive when people would call her fat. However, I could quickly silence the people who felt it was appropriate to comment on her weight by mentioning her thyroid problem. They would go from picking on my little princess to pitying her and getting her a cookie, because *that's* helping matters.

What I never understood is I would never say to anyone, "Are you sure you need to super size that combo because if you eat one more thing, those pants are going to burst." The weight crisis in this country is mind-boggling. Ellen Degeneres is right, when we go to the movies, we stock up on snacks like we're crossing the Andes. Portions in restaurants are insanely huge. Really, do we need the *whole* flank of the cow as a serving of steak? Yet God forbid people push their shopping carts that extra twenty feet to the corral and get just a smidge of exercise.

However, if it were not suitable to comment on a person's weight, why would it be acceptable to say anything about my dog's weight? I have eyes. I can see she has a little in the middle. Mind your own business and have a salad. Regardless of her weight, her temperament remained sound; it was just her weight that was of concern. When I would use her for trainings at work, I would introduce her as my dainty, delicate flower. When we would try to entice a dog to test his Invisible Fence® boundaries, we would "race" across the customer's yard. To define race in this instance, I mean plod along at a sound barrier breaking speed of 0.4 miles per hour. Unless food is involved, Aurora does not feel the need to move with any sense of purpose, or for that matter, move.

There are days I feel brave and let her stay uncrated while I'm at work and when I pull into my parking place in our driveway, I see her head pop up from over the couch. God knows she's not going to get up and see who is pulling down the driveway. Well, let's clarify, she knows my car and isn't going to get up unless she has to pee. When the UPS man shows up, she is defending her house like a true Bullmastiff, and she may let you in, but she isn't letting you out.

At her annual exam, she was given a relatively clean bill of health but her weight was pushing maximum density and for her breed, we needed to be mindful that excess weight is hard on her joints. Dr. Dutton didn't feel that chest, pelvic, or spine x rays were necessary. I requested the usual well care profile of blood-work: complete blood cell count, kidney, liver, glucose levels etc. I also asked that her thyroid be checked just because I couldn't seem to get her to lose weight. She was getting a meager 1-cup of low calorie food in the morning and a mound of raw, meaty bones for dinner. I had cut back her munchkin intake to only one when she was at work with me. How is it she was still such a moose?

A few days later, the results of her blood work were in: hypothyroidism. Again, it is not a big deal in dogs, it really, really isn't. It truly is a matter of thyroid hormone replacement medication and bi-annual screenings to make sure the levels are within normal limits. I however, did not take it well. I wrapped around my little girl that night and was inconsolable. Was this the beginning of her decline? Her whiskers had started to gray, and she didn't have the stamina to go for more than a 30-minute walk in the woods anymore. We were supposed to go to a Godsmack concert that night, but I just couldn't bear to leave my dog. She came to work with me for the next few days because I didn't want to be away from her.

After trial and error of medication levels for four months, her thyroid was regulated and life was happy again. She lost 20 pounds and looked absolutely fabulous. Her waist was defined, she had a spring in her step, and her energy level had returned. Even her chiropractor, Dr. Ham, was thrilled at her weight loss and just how magnificent she looked. I was beaming with pride because of the success story Aurora had become.

At her annual appointment the following year, she had lost even more weight but still looked great. We ran the same blood work profiles, and all her levels came back within normal limits, including her thyroid. However, a few weeks later, her behavior changed drastically.

After Denali died four months prior, she had become more protective of me. It was as if the two of them had an agreement when he was alive: He was the first line of defense in the event of danger, and she was his back up. Danger in this case can be described as a stranger coming down the driveway, the people who like to discuss religion that go door to door to do so, or a leaf. He would go charging at the windows if he felt my safety was in jeopardy (usually translated into a squirrel was in the yard) and she would remain on her couch waiting for her cue to come to action. It rarely came. We had a saying when Denali was alive: "If you can break into our house while the dogs aren't in their crates, you've impressed me. But you're not getting past D. And if you do manage to get by Denali, you still have to contend with Big Mama. But you will never get to me." I didn't feel we needed a security system; I had 330 pounds of protection. So after Denali died, she resumed her role of primary guard dog, being that the other two stooges rarely provided a front line of defense. It was back on the shoulders of Big Mama to keep me safe.

Prior to adopting Denali, her role of guard dog was subtle. Unlike Denali who made his presence known immediately and quite honestly, threateningly, Aurora never felt the need to get off her comfortable cushion on the couch just to tell someone she is there. Denali was always on constant patrol. Aurora was always on constant break. If a squirrel was in the yard, so be it. However, she wasn't just going to let anyone come into the house either. When my friend Betsy came over one afternoon, Aurora almost ripped the window grates down making sure Betsy knew Aurora had not been the one to extend the invitation for dinner. However, once you were in the house and she felt you were not a threat or a cheese-dispensing machine, she rarely had a use for you and would retire back to her cushion on the couch before you tried to sit on it.

If the mood wasn't quite right though, she would put herself between the guest and I. She was being subtle in her way of guarding me. You had to go through her to get to me, and it wasn't likely you'd be able to get through her. My friend Brad had come over on his way home from work and she made sure he knew she would enforce a five-foot radius around me. She never growled, curled a lip, or pinned her ears; she was just there, watching every move Brad made. I knew what she was doing, and it was just fine with me.

At first the changes in her behavior were subtle. She used to lie quietly in the back of my car when I brought her to work. Now, she was barking and carrying on when I was working with a customer's dog. She would lunge out the windows when big vehicles went by, or sometimes the sight of a minivan would set her off and she would lunge. She was now getting cranky too. Sometimes she would be in the car and a jogger on the street would cause her to react with barking and lunging. The worst was when she went after my friend's dog but then redirected her anger at Maureen.

It was a benign enough situation, one we had even been in before. We met at the park for our usual stroll. I had all four of my dogs and Maureen had her miniature Poodle, Rocco. Rocco is also known as the Poo or Poodell, yes, you read the correctly, Poodell. Rocco is an exceptional dog, thus he is given an exceptional title, Poodell. Go with it. There was a gate we had to go through to enter the park. The gate itself was closed with a pad lock and chain, but there was an opening about 18 inches wide between the doors we would scoot through. Maureen and Rocco went through the gate first.

Rocco has proximity issues and doesn't like anyone in his space. I don't blame him, neither do I. More than once I have reminded people who were in my space in line at the grocery store that we are not at Disney World, there isn't a ride at the end of the checkout line, get away from me. Being that Aurora was the most sound of the four dogs and least likely to get into Rocco's space, I handed Maureen the leash so I could walk through the gate with the other dogs.

Apparently, Rocco did not want Maureen to be holding her leash and he curled his lip at Aurora. Normally, Aurora would barely acknowledge such a gesture, or at the most give him a look that says, "I crap bigger than you, knock it off." Not this day. Something in Aurora just snapped and she charged at Rocco and she was going to have him for lunch. Maureen got in the middle trying to keep Aurora away from Rocco.

I was still standing on the other side of the fence helplessly watching this event unfurl all the while making a choice in my head: do

I lose control of all four dogs to hopefully gain control of one dog? Well, I can't let this continue since she clearly isn't going to stop and poor Maureen is going to lose this battle soon. As I was about to lunge for Aurora's hind end, she and Maureen shifted and I ended up sending Maureen flying. Aurora then pinned Maureen and was bearing down on her arm. I was able to grab Aurora and hang her in the air, stand on my other dogs' leashes, and then start praying.

First, is Rocco okay? That's right, is the dog all right? Second, since she can actually communicate with me, is Maureen okay? And in the back of my head, "Oh crap. Aurora has crossed a line. Please don't make me put my dog to sleep. Please don't make me put my dog to sleep. Please don't make me put my dog to sleep" As good of a dog trainer I think I am, I cannot work with aggression that has no provocations.

This is why Maureen and I are such good friends: as she was seeing stars and trying not to pass out, we were able to immediately agree we were glad Aurora went after Maureen and never got to the Poo. She also didn't lose her mind on Aurora after she was feeling better and she didn't start screaming about what a bad dog she was. In fact, it was her idea to continue the walk so that Rocco doesn't have a bad last memory of the terrible experience. I wanted to crawl under a rock and die. Here my dog just tried to kill my friend and her dog, and she wants to not only continue the walk, but with that same dog. She is a better person than I. In fact, she wasn't mad per se. Don't get me wrong, neither of us was happy and Maureen even called Jason on her way home from the park to warn him what happened. She wanted to make sure he knew she wasn't mad, and as best he could, he needed to help me not to freak out when I got home. She's one of those rare people who truly understands dog dynamics and no matter how well we train our dogs, they are dogs first, sometimes shit happens.

I went on a full court press to make sure this *never* happened again. Maureen gave me a gift by not at the very least pressing charges, let alone demand she be euthanized. Aurora, and all the dogs for that matter, was in behavioral boot camp. Everyone had to sit for everything. No one was allowed on the furniture. I picked up a few treat puzzles for Aurora to give her mental stimulation. I e-mailed all my vets and trusted trainers to get their opinion and the general consensus was she was probably in pain due to her dual knee surgeries, degenerative joint disease, Spondylosis and basically, she's a 7 year old giant breed dog. She's old, crotchety, and sore. Keep her on a leash, increase her Glucosemine, add an anti-inflammatory such as DGP, keep her out of situations where she might be volatile, and always be ready for the worst. The thing is Aurora was not acting painful in the least. But since I am not a doctor, I did give the advice its proper credence. Then it hit me... Her recent thyroid panel values were normal, but in the low range of normal. Duh!

Maureen, who also suffers from hypothyroidism, concurred that an out of whack thyroid will indeed cause sporadic, cranky, unstable behavior. A few weeks prior, Maureen had gone up one side and down the other of her neighbor whose cat kept pooping in Maureen's yard. Normally, Maureen is my voice of calm, mature reason. I defer to her when I need to express an opinion and need direction on how to do it softly without teeth. She will guide me in a soft, subtle manner, or tell me to just keep my mouth shut and let the cards fall where they may. However, my friend is indeed human, a human with a thyroid problem, and sometimes my friend bites. Among so many reasons, it's why I love her so.

I called Dr. Dutton and he suggested we run a Michigan State University Thyroid panel. We did and the doctor e-mailed me the results a few days later. It was exactly what I needed to hear: her thyroid was shot! It was practically non-existent. Every level was far below the normal range, barely registering at all on the charts. I got the e-mail as I was in the grocery store and I kid you not, I was truly doing the dance of joy in the coffee aisle. Anyone watching was hoping I would pick up the decaffeinated can because clearly I did not need any more caffeine. I immediately called Maureen to let her know. We danced with joy together. Again, I am not excusing my dog's aggression, nor will I ever excuse aggression. However, in this case, I will make an allowance that she had a medical reason for her behavior.

About a week into changing her thyroid medication, she seemed better. She was back to being more even keeled and less edgy and antsy. Before we knew it was her thyroid, in an act of sheer desperation because Aurora was becoming an unpredictable little beast, I called an animal communicator Maureen used and swore by. Fine, what could it hurt? Maureen's reading was so good that even Maureen's husband's relatives popped their noses into the reading saying Craig needed to slow down or he would be joining them in Heaven sooner than anyone would like. Well, gee, I would love to hear from my father that passed away when I was two years old. I would even like a shout out from my Grandmother to let me know she's proud of me. I would *kill* to have just one more conversation with her. Why not call the clairvoyant? Oh, and for $5 more bucks, she tapes the session and mails it to you so what you didn't remember in the session will be repeated back to you. Swell. Sign me up. I was pretty sure we had Aurora's issues resolved, but it would be nice to hear my dog's "voice" say she was feeling better but had felt like crap for a long time.

That being said, let me go on record by stating I *hated* my reading to the point Jason, who was in Indiana at the time, had to scrape me off the ceiling while I was still on the phone with the woman. I was e mailing him as the Miss Cleo knock off was speaking. I was losing my mind and cursing like a sailor at how condescending and snotty she was. Honestly, she didn't tell me anything I didn't know. I was fine with that aspect.

The kicker, and this is what sent me over the edge, was she insinuated that Rora sleeping upstairs with us in our bedroom was contributing to her demise by having her go up and down the stairs to be with us. It was, in fact, *killing* her to go up and down the stairs. In addition, I was already compromising Porter's health by having him use stairs as well. I would be doing all my dogs a favor by having them sleep on the first floor. She stated they are just dogs and they will adapt to the change.

Are you kidding me? *Just dogs?* My dogs are not *just dogs.* Dogs are *pack animals.* I know plenty of people who don't allow their dogs upstairs and if that works for them that is fine with me. That's not how it is in *my* house, and how other people live is of no true concern to me. But dogs truly are pack animals and want to be in the den with the rest of their pack. Killian has slept *in the bed* with us since we got him 7 years ago. He is the dog who gets in the bed and warms up my spot for me while I'm brushing my teeth. Tatum does the midnight creep into our bed every night and uses my ankle as a pillow. Porter has been my shadow since he came to live with us when he was 7 months old and he sleeps on his bed right next to me. Now you want me to leave them downstairs? That would *crush* my dogs. I haven't gone to the bathroom alone in seven years. They would have no understanding why they couldn't be within a 3-foot proximity of me.

It was all I could do not to tell this woman off. Aurora is a guard dog, it is her job to make sure I am safe, a job she takes very seriously. Her bed is between the door and our bed so she can protect me. As another aside for those of you who have your dogs sleep elsewhere, Aurora had a seizure at 4:00 one morning. It lasted about 45 seconds. She has never had another seizure and nothing in her history would give an indication as to why she had this seizure. However, if she had been downstairs, away from me, I never would have known she had a seizure. For the next six months, I would wake up from 3:30 to 4:30 and just listen to her breathe.

Aurora does not want to sleep down stairs, and she can maneuver the stairs just fine, thank you very much. When I got the tape, I had Jason listen to it being that he isn't the protective mother bear with her cubs that I am and he tends to have a better voice of reason than say, oh, I don't know, me. At first, he was in agreement with Rasputen's protégé in that she was "reading" Rora when her thyroid was all out of sorts and Aurora was indeed a cranky pants. Fine, I will make that allowance. But as the tape progressed, Jason would turn it off every few minutes and actually argue with it that she was so wrong and interjecting her own opinion about how we should now care for our dogs, and **no one** was going to tell him how to raise his dogs except, well... me. I felt truly vindicated in my rage from the week before. I was grinning ear to ear and sending an eternal extended middle finger to this woman.

For grins, we tried an experiment that night to see what Rora would do if we gave her the choice of sleeping downstairs away from us just to see if the Sooth Sayar possibly had a point. Everyone else went upstairs like they were supposed to when we went upstairs to go to bed. Mama stayed on her couch in the living room with a look of "you go on up. I'm comfy and content". Okay. As you wish, my feelings are hurt but okay.

Around 2:00, she came upstairs and demanded to be let out to potty. Aurora is unlike most dogs that will whimper or scratch to go out. Not my Big Girl. She squares off, braces herself and SHOUTS that she needs to potty. You can feel the breeze hit your face from the strength of her lungs expelling air. I'm not a big fan of my dog telling me what to do but I'm even less of a fan of crap on my carpet at 2:00 in the morning. I got up and let the dogs out since everyone had to join in for the fun. For the record, she went down the stairs without a problem, I'm just saying. She went outside, poops and pees and goes back to her couch in the living room, which, by the way, she hopped up on without even a wince. Fine. I go up the stairs to go to bed with the rest of the dogs, and again, I'm a little hurt but this is her choice.

The rest of us go upstairs and go back to bed. Around 4:00, she comes back upstairs; again, without incident I might add. She does her guttural growl and boots Killian off the papazan chair just by looking at him, because she can. But doesn't get on it. She goes to the foot of our bed, looks around and surveys her kingdom, wags her tail, and bounds up on our bed with an "oh yeah. I'm back," look on her face, circles twice, lies down, and goes to sleep. I silently said to myself, "You know what Honey; you deserve it, sweet dreams Big Girl."

# In Case of Emergency

We've all filled out the In Case of Emergency forms, and there's nothing more that states you're an adult then when you can actually list someone other than your mom as said contact. The form is at our doctor's office. There's one where we work. If you have children, there is one at their school. If you go away on vacation and board your dogs, you leave that information at the boarding facility. In my case, I don't have one emergency contact, I have five, but that's just me. You never know when someone won't be home.

My friend Megan had let me know there was a form you could put in your glove compartment of your car to let the paramedics know what your wishes are for your dogs in case you are incapacitated, yet your dogs are not. This will prevent the attending police officers or medical professionals from bringing your dogs to the local shelter and will provide an emergency contact number for someone who will come get your pets in the event of an emergency. Swell. Sign me up.

It wasn't two weeks earlier I had been elated to learn the Progressive Insurance Company offers coverage for your pets in the event of an auto accident. I called my insurance agent, who by all accounts is wonderful. He informed me our insurance company doesn't offer that coverage. I hinted that I would hate to cancel our policy and leave because my dogs aren't allowed coverage but if I had a child, the child would be covered. My dogs *are* my children. I want coverage for my dogs if I have that option. I was quickly crushed when I learned that no insurance company in New Hampshire offered coverage for pets, including Progressive. However, life is about perspective, I truly feel when one door closes, a window of opportunity opens.

Enter my friend Megan with her ICE form. If they can't get insurance protection, at least they could have a "voice" of direction in the event of an emergency. As I am filling out the form, a feeling of dread overcomes me. This form is to be kept in the glove compartment. It occurred to me what a disastrous situation that could be. That would require someone to not only get into the car, but be allowed in the car long enough to rescue me, restrain my dogs, which by all accounts, would be easier to do before trying to rescue me, and then find the form. Riiiiiiiiiiiiiiight. Somehow I don't see that happening.

A few weeks prior, we had been at the gas station. Porter was quickly becoming a dog that deemed my car as his and it was his personal responsibility to keep anyone and everyone away from the vehicle. He was losing his mind over the man at the gas pump next to us who, as threatening as could be, was sitting still in his vehicle listening to his radio while his friend was inside paying for the gas. Porter was growling and snapping and being a real brat. This then provoked the other dogs to start barking at anything so there was now a wonderful chorus of chaos coming from my truck. I think the man next to us felt it would be wise to keep his eyes forward and not acknowledge the mêlée occurring immediately to his left. Jason came back from the store and asked what the fuss was about.

"The man in the car next to us had the audacity to stay in his car while we were parked here. Porter felt that wasn't a good choice," I replied.

Jason knows when one dog barks, the rest join in, even if they don't know why, and whether you want them to or not. We both agreed that *clearly* that man made a bad choice and Porter was just trying to keep the world safe by thwarting radio listeners.

Jason and I had "joked" more than once over the last few years that if we were to be pulled over by a police officer and had Denali in the car, we would have no choice to but to get out of our vehicle and go sit in the squad car while the officer checked our licenses and criminal records. We wouldn't want the poor police officer to feel that pulling out a weapon or mace was necessary because there would be a slim chance in Hades that Denali would allow anyone to reach toward the vehicle to take my license and registration. Porter was quickly assuming a position Denali had left open after he passed.

We were doing our best to try and curb that behavior. Instead of using harsh tones to correct Porter's behavior, we tried using happy excited voices to change Porter's perception of the situation. If we are happy someone is approaching the car, we can encourage Porter to be happy to make a new friend. Sometimes he bought it, sometimes he didn't. He is a work in progress on so many levels.

I filled out the ICE with great detail. I didn't have one emergency contact. I had five. In fact, I made a note stating it might be better to call more than one contact so that the dogs could go to different people since four dogs were a lot for any one person to handle. Now that I think about it, I should probably update that list to have my mother be the one who delegates which dog goes where. Again, we're back to having our mothers be the primary point of contact in an emergency. I felt obligated at the bottom of the ICE form to include the following: OUR DOGS ARE FRIENDLY BUT

THEY ARE PROTECTIVE.  PROCEED SLOWLY AND WITH TREATS.

I could see it now.  I'm slumped over the steering wheel and Porter is barking and snapping at everyone within a 20-foot radius of the car.  Aurora is putting herself between me and anyone who tries to come near me; even if that means standing *on* me, severed artery and all.   Tatum, who had a meltdown the other day when we went through the car wash because she was certain we were under attack, is now cowering in the back terrified by all the commotion and is now baring her teeth at anyone who gingerly reaches for her.  Killian, well, bless his heart, he's everyone's best friend.  I'm in trouble.

# FROSTY THE SNOWMAN

As Porter's confidence blossomed, so did his guard dog instincts. He started off as a shy little boy. We did the usual things to socialize him. We sent him to doggie daycare to learn social skills and how to play well with other dogs. We enrolled in an obedience class to continue to develop his obedience and social skills. I know they are supposed to say it, but our dogs truly are favorites among the staff at Brookwood Pet Report, or at least that's what they told me and that's what I believe. But I mean really, what's not to love?

While I certainly feel no one physically abused Porter when he was living in the pet store before he was turned over to Bordeaux Rescue, I don't think anyone took the time to *love* him. As a result, new situations scare him. New people make him nervous, especially men. And God forbid someone drop a book, he heads for the hills, tail tucked and ears pinned. We do our best to comfort him in these situations and not over coddle him when he is being oversensitive about nothing. We arm people with treats so Porter feels comfortable in both the situation as well as meeting a new person. And we make fun, silly jokes with high-pitched voices when he seems nervous to help redirect his drama to something positive. He feels better, and we look foolish. Seems like a fair trade.

Maureen and I were snowshoeing in the park with Rocco, Porter, Tatum, and Killian one particular winter day when we crossed the path of two men who appeared to be of questionable nature. Granted, we are in New Hampshire and I don't expect people to be in their Armani suits for tea and crumpets when they are in the woods. These men were in their flannel John Boy shirts, wrangler jeans, and Skoal tins in their pockets. In and of itself, that sight isn't a rarity, but there was 2 feet of fresh snow on the ground and yet they were there with their Ford Tempo, not exactly the cars for a leisurely drive in the woods in two feet of snow. The parking lot where they were parked was the same parking lot Maureen and I had been doing donuts in when we got to the park two hours prior enjoying the fresh powder. I've been stuck in the snow in a Tempo before. It wouldn't be my first choice of transport on anything other than a clear, dry, paved road on a clear, sunny day with a cell phone that had a full range of signal bars and a fully charged battery.

As we approached the men, Porter started his guttural growling. I was about to tell him to knock it off when they started talking to us. Oh, now to know me is to love me, and everyone knows I am like my dogs; I don't like anyone until given a reason to. I'm not on this walk to make friends with anyone except the company in which I keep. As it turned out, Maureen did a better job running interference than I would have. Instead of seizing this opportunity to show Porter not all strangers are bad, we embraced it as a "stay the heck away from us" lesson. Well, Maureen did, and I didn't object.

The man asked if Porter would bite. Before I could answer, Maureen very matter of factly stated he would not bite, so long as they stayed right where they were and didn't come any closer. We pass by them without any further incident and load the dogs into our trucks that are parked about one hundred feet away. I have no idea what possessed Maureen, but at that moment, she decided to clean the excess snow off the top of her Jeep. I felt inclined to not only stay behind with her to make sure she was not kidnapped and killed, but to then pick on her for her oddly timed decision. We narrowly escaped dismemberment by the Clough Park hoodlums, but now you tease the bad men with your snowbrush? My dogs are good, but they don't protect the moronic.

But lest you think we let my dogs growl at every new comer into our line of vision, we try to redirect rude behavior and also try to teach bravery. Her dog Rocco needs his routine. If something is out of the ordinary, he becomes suspect. His dinner is served religiously at 5:00 PM. Should a situation arise and his dinner is not ready until 5:15, he starts pawing at Maureen and pacing into the kitchen as if the Dinner Fairy will magically appear and serve him his dinner. If an object is out of place, he knows, even if we don't, that it must have been placed there by aliens and at any moment that object is going to kill us all and he then rises to the call of protective duty by barking and pointing. Maureen and I have stopped numerous times and talked to misplaced objects along the trails in the woods to reassure Rocco that all is well. There was a hubcap that was in the middle of the trail that probably fell off the previously mentioned Tempo and it was in the cross hairs of Rocco's alarm. We stopped our walk so we could carefully examine the hubcap and after five minutes of discussion, we assured Rocco that the hubcap could indeed pose a trip hazard, but beyond that, it was a minimal threat. We were able to continue our walk knowing we had thwarted the hubcap leaving aliens and mankind was safe.

During a subsequent walk, someone had built a snowman along the trail. He was indeed a lovely snowman, although he did not come dressed with a corncob pipe, an old top hat, nor did he have two eyes made of coal. Perhaps it was those lack of adornments that provoked our little Porter. I noticed Porter's stance had changed from goofy oaf to on guard. I looked ahead to see what he was zeroing in on. When I spotted the lovely ice sculpture, the growling commenced.  As I said, he knows he's a guard dog; he's just not sure from what I do and don't need guarding.  What was also upsetting, in Porter's mind, was that none of the other dogs had made notice of the snowman so now our safety was in his paws since no one else was stepping up to the plate.

At this point, Maureen and I took this opportunity to show Porter that Frosty was a good snowman, a jolly soul if you will.  We sat down and talked to Frosty to further demonstrate the benefits of having a snowman as a friend.  We patted the snowman.  Porter's whiskers extended to "touch" the snowman, his neck fully extended as far as it could go while still standing two feet from the snowman, and he immediately recoiled upon feeling cold on his whiskers.  Then he let his nose touch the snowman to sniff it and again, he jumped back.

We were still carrying on like fools to encourage bravery.  We were talking in high pitched, squeaky tones.  We were rubbing the snowman to continue to show him the opportunities that exist with Frosty as a friend.  The goal is to show Porter that he can meet new people, those of flesh and blood as well as those of frozen water rolled into 3 balls that stand three feet high, and not feel threatened.  As if to further demonstrate the benign nature of Frosty, Rocco came up and peed on Frosty.  We are currently waiting to see if the last part of the lesson carries on to the next meet n greet situation.

# CHICKEN OF THE SEA

I was fortunate when we adopted Killian. I was able to meet his former owners and get a brief medical history. The Good Samaritan that hit him with his truck brought him immediately to us at the animal hospital. It might have had something to do with the fact Killian jumped right into his truck when the man got out to see if the pooch was OK. He was by no means OK, but he was going to be fine. The man offered to keep Killian if no one claimed him or wanted him, but I was already in love. New Hampshire state law states if no one comes to claim a dog after 7 days, he is fair game for adoption. It was literally the 6th day and 12th hour when Killian's owners showed up at the hospital and he was definitely their dog.

As it turned out, I knew this dog and loved him before he was mine. He would board at the animal hospital occasionally while his family was on vacation and he was so sweet and wonderful. He had become one of my favorites then and he had quickly become a huge part of my heart in those six days since his accident. Now here was his real mom and four kids here to see him. I was crushed. I had already bought him a crate for the condominium on the rare instance he wasn't with me when I went somewhere, a crate for my SUV, toys, bowls, and even a monogrammed bed.

The relief veterinarian that was temporarily working at the Animal Hospital for Killian's original treatment discussed Killian's injuries with his owner. Dr. Hoffheimer pulled out the x-rays and showed the extensive damage to his pelvis. Killian was already 5 years old and would definitely develop crippling arthritis at an early age. Then I came forward, tears in my eyes at the thought of possibly losing my new best friend, and we discussed what I was already doing in terms of caring for him as he recovered from his injuries. I was carrying him up the stairs at my condo, I had started him on Glucosemine and Chondroiton supplements to help offset arthritis as long as possible, and since I get a very good discount on services and products, if hip replacement is necessary, I have the means to provide the surgery, as well as the time and commitment to care for him as he recovers.

The mother agreed he was badly injured, and then almost in an attempt to convince herself she was making the right choice, she started telling me his problems, one being he takes off all the time. I assured her we live in a condominium community that has a leash requirement for dogs. She told me Killian has Pancreatitis and has a very tender tummy. Again, all things I promised to care for in earnest and when he has flare ups, he can come to work with me. They agreed to release him to me and my life had forever been changed for the better as I had been touched by this little furry angel.

Being that I worked at an animal hospital, I was surrounded by brands of Science Diet and just assumed if my vet was carrying it, it was the top of the line, best of the best dog food. There are certainly worse foods out there, and you definitely need some of those prescription foods for various medical issues. However, the over the counter brands of Science Diet do not agree with my Killian. We determined he is allergic to corn, a main ingredient in many Science Diet as well as many other medium grade foods. He had chronic ear infections. But the really fun part was every six weeks, Killian would blow with pure liquid, eye watering, nostril burning diarrhea. It would then last for two to three weeks. This went on for six months. The development of "I'm not leaving my wingman" started here, because if Killian was sick, all plans were canceled, including lunch with my mom, and he didn't leave my sight.

Anyone who has had a dog with an upset tummy knows the bland diet drill. Boiled hamburger or chicken and white rice for a week and then slowly introduce the dog's regular food over the next week. Now I truly would lay in traffic for my dog, but I hate to cook. When Jason and I were first married, I really did have more take out places than friends in my cell phone address book. I hate to cook. It makes me cranky.

One morning I had a craving for scrambled eggs. I love scrambled eggs, especially with cheese in them. However, we didn't have any milk. Not to be discouraged though, I discovered we did have Creamora milk substitute for coffee. I thought, "hey, it works in my coffee, it should work in my eggs, right?" Wrong. I don't think joint compound is as thick as the paste I created with that culinary concoction. Nevertheless, I did learn a valuable lesson and I am now sharing it with you. When without milk, water is a better choice for making scrambled eggs.

Moving on. So here I was, in the grocery store for the millionth time getting bland food ingredients for my dog, and I was lost. It baffles me that the same chain of groceries stores have different set ups for where they keep the same products. Being that my attention to detail is nihil, no matter what I put on my resume, even attention to the big picture can confuse me, which is why what should be a 5-minute shopping trip is usually no less than a 30-minute event.

Suddenly, during this latest shopping event, I came across the canned tuna aisle. Slightly to the left was a small section that had low fat, low sodium canned chicken. I had an epiphany and was in heaven. I stocked up like the great canned chicken famine was coming. I grabbed the economy-sized box of minute rice and I was on my way as elated as if I had won the canned chicken lottery. One cup of rice and one can of chicken had a prep time of five minutes, most of which was spent waiting for the water to boil in the microwave. No mess. No clean up. And most importantly, there was no cooking.

One morning, I was running late for work and it was during one of Killian's bouts of diarrhea. I had enough time to get to work and make Killian's breakfast at work, put him in an indoor run in the boarding kennel wing of the hospital, and not be late for my shift. My coworker was busy doing the morning kennel shift when she saw what I was doing and she got a very puzzled look on her face.

"Michelle, does Killian like tuna?"

I had no idea where she was going with this but I answered with a quick, "I don't know," and kept going about my business because I had less than 5 minutes to feed my dog and be at the front desk.

Jan repeated her question, "Michelle, are you sure Killian likes tuna?"

"I really have no idea," and this time I had tone in my voice because I was really scrambling to get him fed and not be late and I didn't have time for chit chat about what Killian does and doesn't like for seafood cuisine.

"Well you're feeding him tuna."

I look down at the can and it clearly says chicken on it so I hold up the can and say with possibly more tone, "No I'm not, it says chicken right here."

She takes the can from me and points to it, "Of the Sea."

Oops.

*Aurora says, "Go! No Really Go!"*

*Aurora says, "You're not funny."*

*Aurora with her pillows.*

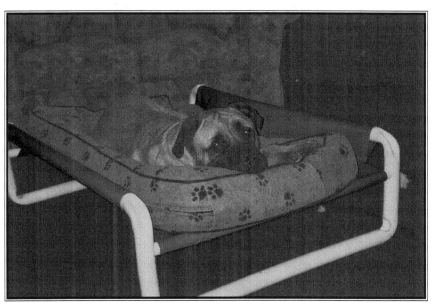

*Aurora after a hard day of relaxing.*

*Christmas Killian*

*Denali in the pumpkins.*

*Happy Killian.*

*Killian says, "Faster!"*

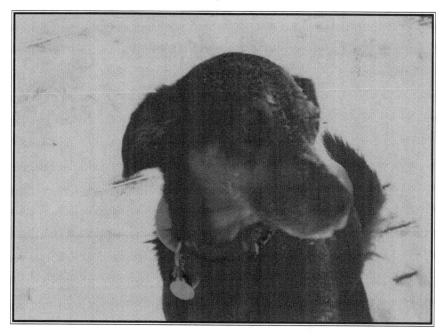

*Killian's snow profile.*

*Porter and Killian at the lake.*

*Porter - "Look into my eyes."*

*Tatum and Aurora share a bone*

*Tatum - "Where are we going?"*

*Tatum with her puzzle.*

*Tatum's close up.*

# Daycare

I swear to Christmas, if it's not nailed down, Tatum will eat it. There's a restriction on her insurance policy that will not cover obstructions because stupid me, I got the policy after she obstructed. In my defense, I got it because when she obstructed, she was 1 year old. Good gravy, if she's going to obstruct this early in life, she will do it again, if not just to spite me. Now it's considered a "pre existing condition." Personally, I consider mange to be a pre existing condition, or even Pancreatitis, but at the very least something *medical* to be a condition that exists prior to a policy being written. I do not, however, consider eating a cardboard box until you vomit in my shoes a condition per se, no more so than I consider biting one's fingernails a habit, not something that gets a person placed in the "take two of these and call me in the morning" category.

We found that on the days she attended daycare, she was calmer, relaxed, less of an imp to the rest of the dogs, she wasn't trying to cram every object that was on the floor into her mouth, and harmony existed in my house. We started bringing her to daycare when she was just twelve weeks old to get the socialization process underway. I usually brought her on my days off so I could enjoy my day off without finding a piddle puddle on the carpet, or wondering what she ate now only to find out through regurgitation, usually in the middle of the night.

It was daycare day and come Hell or high water, I will have an appropriately socialized Pit Bull. I'm a dog trainer for crying out loud. How embarrassing would that be? Jason earned his way into sainthood that winter. I was still a newbie at the Canine Fence Company and therefore on the low end of the pay scale. In an effort to afford her daycare, we had to make sacrifices elsewhere in the budget. Obviously, the correct choice was our own food quality would have to go by the wayside. Even though the dogs were getting the high quality foods that had main ingredients like salmon and bison, in order to afford those foods and daycare, Jason and I ate those meals from a box where you just add water and cook at 400 degrees for 45 minutes. I think salt licks have less sodium and I don't want to know what grade of "chicken" was in the casserole, but Tatum's social skills were worth it.

When Tatum was still quite small, she made it very clear after her breakfast one morning she wanted nothing more than to go back to bed. I put everyone in the crates and found Tatum curled on the couch, half under a blanket practically snoring. Until my dogs start kicking in for the mortgage, if I want them to do something, chop chop, let's go. I picked her up, let her snuggle in my coat, and off we went.

She really is a petite little dog and when she was a puppy, I could put her in my lap and drive with one knee as I typed on my blackberry while I drove to the pet resort. When I turned off the car, she barely opened one eye. She barely looked at me with an expression of "Oh, I can't possibly be expected to... Hey... (sniff sniff) What's that smell? Where am I?" She lifted her head and was wide-awake. She knew exactly where we were and couldn't get out of the car fast enough. I had a hard time getting her leash on her and barely grabbed her teething bone, Mr. Chewy. She launched into the arms of Mark, the manager of playgroup, and I didn't get so much as a look back as she bounded into the day care room. She loved it there and they loved having her there.

Porter was slower to warm up to the playgroup scenario. In fact, the first time we brought him to Brookwood, we naturally brought Tatum with him so she could show him how much fun it was there and there was nothing to fear. Being the nerds that we are, we even took a picture of him by the sign for Brookwood Pet Resort for his first day of school. We got into the lobby and Tatum promptly left him in the dust as she bombed into the day camp room barking at the top of her lungs letting everyone know there is a new doggie sheriff in town. He heard the barking of the other dogs and immediately, his tail was touching his chin by way of his belly and even though Jason had his leash, he was clawing at the tile floor in vain trying to get to me. It was like he was having a pet store flash back. "MOOOOOOOOOOOOOOOOOOOOMMM-MMMMMMMMMMMMMMMM. DON'T LEEEEEEEEEEE-AAAAAAAAAAAAAAVVVVVVVVVVVEEEEEEEE MEEEEE EEEEEEEEEEEEEEEEEEEEEEEEEEEEEEEEEEEEEEEEEEEEE." Not only did we get the look back as he went into the daycare bunk room for dogs, we got the desperate attempts to flee the hands of Mark and get to us.

The report in the afternoon was he would circle the dogs as they played but never engaged. Even though it had been a while since Tatum was in daycare due to my work schedule exploding that spring, she was in the mix of everything, letting everyone know she was back and it was her world, welcome to it. She was there to reclaim her title of Queen Beast.

The following week was a similar departure. I still got the pathetic look back from Porter, and a mere flash of Tatum's butt as she slipped through the door. The report at the end of the day was more promising though. He would engage ever so slightly, but then retreat. Progress is progress. I'll take it. As the weeks progressed, he gained confidence and was now a card-carrying member of the Doggie Day Camp program and no longer needs his Momma when he's being dropped off. In fact, I'm pretty sure he and Tatum would prefer it if I would drop them off at the end of the street so they wouldn't have to be seen with me. If you think dogs don't act like teenagers too, you're wrong.

After a few months of regular sessions at Daycare, I picked up Porter and Tatum and was told they both did well in playgroup for the day. I always ask how they did and always get the same answer, they did fine. I keep waiting for a more detailed description like Tatum cured cancer or Porter split the atom. But as long as I leave with 2 dogs that have all eight of their legs, I'll consider it a win.

One week, I was driving home after picking them up and Porter was helping me drive by blocking my view of the rearview mirror and putting his massive head on my shoulder. I saw Porter had scrapes on his head. A lot of scrapes on his head. I immediately call Brookwood and was told Mark and Carol had gone home, but they would leave a note and someone would call me in the morning. When we got home, I thoroughly inspected him and found just the scrapes, but no puncture wounds that required sutures and I was holding off calling the plastic surgeon. For now.

The next morning, Carol e mailed me. She had checked with Mark and the scrapes on Porter came from Tatum. It seems that every week, our little Imp is always in the center of the playgroup and she jumps out at everyone who passes by. She is the same way at home, why should playgroup be any different? In this particular case, Porter's head was in the direct path of Tatum's teeth. A perfectly rational explanation.

The next week, Jason picked up the dogs from daycare. The kennel staff warned him that this time when Tatum came out, she had a boo-boo. He had called me to warn me before I got home that she had a boo-boo. "Define boo-boo," I said. No one saw it happen but she definitely had a scratch on her head and maybe she hit it in her crate during naptime.

Now, please don't mistake me for being a complete idiot. I'm over the top about my dogs, that I am fully aware of, and even I know it is daycare. In fact, it's daycare for *dogs*. I get it, crap happens. But when I looked at Tatum that evening, and I got a close up view because she was sacked out in my lap all night as we watched TV, she did not have an, "Ow I hit my head," mark on her head. She had a puncture wound with an inch long scratch down her forehead, from a tooth. It's fair to say I was less than calm.

I was seething. Tatum is not the type of girl who will willingly let someone chew on her head. She is a tenacious terrier. If you bite her, she will bite you back. I spent the night obsessing about what could have happened. If someone's dog put a hole in my dog, there's a good chance she will put a hole in another dog. And since she is a Pit Bull, few will give me the benefit of the doubt that someone else started pushing her buttons. She loves her playgroup. I was worried the staff might have to ask her to leave at another client's request. My mother's dog was kicked out of daycare because he is an absolute pushy bully and would try to dominate every dog in his group. However, because he's a Schnauzer, his bad behavior is dismissed. I don't have that luxury with the breeds I own. In my head, I was going over and over how no one saw a dog chewing on my dog.

I was still pretty upset the next morning when I was getting ready for work. She, on the other hand, was no worse for the wear. She was bombing around, playing Nascar, nipping at Porter and jumping over Killian with her "catch me if you can" gleam in her eye. Then it occurred to me that perhaps it wasn't a matter of someone not paying attention to the dogs playing. As she made her 5th loop around the house, Aurora had joined the game in her usual way. She laid in the middle of the floor as the dogs ran by her and opened her mouth like an alligator in the Serengeti waiting for a gazelle to jump into harm's way. She even makes that sound from deep within her throat like an alligator.

Since Tatum was a ringleader, and she was known to move at lightening speed, this thought crossed my mind since no one saw an altercation between her and another dog that there *wasn't* a fight. Maybe, and this is just a suggestion, that perhaps, there is a chance, the possibility if you will, there could be the probability that, again, maybe, she managed to run by a dog who, possibly, had his mouth open and perhaps, her head collided with an exposed canine tooth and there is the slight chance she never even stopped to say "Ouch." I'm just throwing that out there as a possible theory as to why she had a hole on her head that is now a possible candidate for plastic surgery.

# A Fire Hydrant Kind of Day

At 1:30 on a stormy Monday morning, Tatum is in her bed and starts crying. It is not her usual "I have to pee," cry, which she doesn't do anyway, but what else was it going to be at that ungodly hour? Jason and I do our usual Rock Paper Scissors to see who has to get up and let her out. He loses. By no means does that mean I fall back to sleep. As a rule, I lie in bed and listen to make sure nothing happens since clearly a man of his intelligence and aptitude just might not be able to turn a doorknob and open a door to let a dog outside to go to the bathroom. But I'm still in bed nice and warm, so I consider it a win.

Jason gets up to let her out, but not only will she not get off her bed, she won't go down the stairs. She stands at the top of the stairs, imploring him to help her with her eyes as wide and pathetic as can be, but he can't figure out what she wants. He carries the beast down the stairs and puts her outside, except she won't move off the steps. It's pouring, and she just stands there, again, shivering and pitifully looking for help. She ends up peeing on the steps and comes back inside. She then stands at the bottom of the stairs so then Jason has to carry her *back* up the stairs. As he lifts her, she cries in pain. He puts her down next to my side of the bed and she's crying still. I asked him to get a towel so she could sleep with me but I don't want to get the bed wet, or myself for that matter. I'm sympathetic, but I certainly don't want to be uncomfortable. Then she jumps on the bed with me and really yipes so something is truly bothering the little Tatum Bellerina. She nestles in my neck and whimpers herself to sleep.

Now I know something is wrong because she used to sleep like that when she was just a puppy. When she was about 8 months old, and she raked her claws down my face one night while she was sleeping, she was banished from our bed and had her own dog bed. On the floor. Like a Common *Dog*. She did not feel she should muck around on the floor like regular canines, in Steerage Class if you will. However, we created that monster and to this day, she will ever so delicately creep into our bed in the middle of the night and maneuver her way under the covers. She will then sleep with her head resting on my ankle and her toes are usually kicking me in the bum. This night, though, she spent the rest of that night curled right into me, as pathetic as she could be.

The next morning she was still crying and wouldn't go up or down stairs. I had to carry her down the stairs and the act of picking her up caused her to scream. Due to the monsoon we were having that morning, I had been placed on the drive hold for work until 10:00. I took that opportunity to bring her to the animal hospital. Again, I pledge my undying gratitude for the staff at Weare Animal Hospital because when I called to make the appointment, my voice was quivering, I was told to bring her on down right away.

I carried her into the office because yes, she's still being pathetic. As I delicately place her on the floor, she cried. We walked to the sitting area and she yiped with every step. At least the staff is seeing what I'm seeing and that I'm not over dramatizing this symptom, but with every yipe she lets out, I worry she has severed her spinal cord. The doctor did a couple flexing maneuvers with her and came to a quick conclusion. She pulled out her back. She most likely did it while dreaming about being a beast because she was fine when she went to bed. Why am I the only person I know that these things happen to? No really. Why?

$160 later, she got an injection of pain medication, muscle relaxers, and anti inflammatories. We were barely out of the parking lot and she was zonked out in the back seat of my car. I was about 2 miles down the road and I had to check to make sure she was breathing. She was breathing just fine and I was relieved that her pain was being managed. Her cries are more pitiful than most and it kills me to hear her cry.

I pulled into the driveway with a sense of relief that the little Imp was going to live and to my surprise a giant tree is now lying across the front of the darn driveway. Great. Now I have to carry the Princess of Pathetic down my driveway since she was in no condition to walk, just drool. One thing I love about our house is we are set back very far from the road and have quite a bit of privacy. However, in times like these, or blizzards, the privacy and snow become a drawback, as the driveway is a quite long. We get in to the house and I bring her bed downstairs to the living room with her fleece blanket and fleece pillow and tuck her in. She sacks out and goes to sleep.

After an hour, it was almost time for me leave for work. I had spent the last 30 minutes trying to cancel the appointment because I knew the customer's dog wasn't going to want to work in previously mentioned torrential rain. No luck. The customer wasn't home. Ten minutes before I need to leave, we lost power. We sometimes heat our house using a wood pellet stove. Being that it was 35 degrees and raining, it was rather cold out thus requiring heat in the house. The pellet stove had been running all morning. For those of you who aren't burdened with heating a house, the way a pellet stove works is it generates a fire within the stove. A fan blows the heat into the house and an exhaust fan blows the smoke out of the house. Power is required to run both of those fans. Without power, the fire just burns the pellets within the stove and smoke fills the house. Guess what happened when the power went out.

I called my office and said, "I'll go to my appointment, but I'm going to be late because I need to make sure my house doesn't catch on fire because oh, by the way, there is that giant tree still at the front of the driveway so should my house catch on fire, no one can come rescue my dogs… Or sweaters. Or shoes." My coworker laughed and said when I got there, I got there and not to worry. The fire eventually went out, smoke completely filled my now cold house, and I was now officially cranky. The warmth that the pellet stove had created was now gone because I had to open the windows to circulate the smoke out of the house.

But wait, there's more. Getting back to the driveway for a moment. Since we live in the middle of a hill, we have a few culverts that run under our driveway for drainage purposes. As I was bringing Tatum back to the house, one culvert was obviously not draining properly. The water was getting dangerously close to cresting the driveway thus washing it away creating yet another issue should my house decide to catch on fire. I called Jason for what is now the fourth time since deciding to bring Tatum to the hospital. I was trying to really impress upon him he needs to get home and take care of the calamity of drama that is ensuing our house. I was OK with the tree across the driveway, but I would like to continue to *have* a driveway and since he knows how to operate the backhoe tractor and I don't, his presence was required to unplug the culvert. He was unable to leave work early and we would just have to hope for the best.

I went to my appointment that ended up canceling due to the down pouring rain as I was pulling into their driveway. I went back home and found everything as I left it:

- Tree across the driveway. Check.

- A raging river about to crest the driveway and wash it away. Check.

- Unconscious Pit Bull in the living room. Check.

- A cold house that still reeks of smoke. Check.

Jason came right home after work even though I had been pressing for him to come home since discovering the tree across the driveway. He was able to remove the tree and unplugged the culvert. Tatum started showing signs of life and was moving around. She would stop and check every so often just to see if we were watching her to make sure we were seeing how brave she was being and to let us know how close to death she had been just a few hours ago. We lit a couple candles to remove the smoke smell and we managed to have an enjoyable evening.

We greet another day the following morning. Tatum shows no signs of being injured in the least. For $160, she could at least limp for a few days. Humor me. Jason and I both go to work, business as usual. I had a break in the day between appointments and I went home to let the dogs out for potty.

I walked into the house and was greeted with that familiar smell of something not quite right. It wasn't bad trash. It wasn't rancid chicken... I rounded the corner into the dogs' room. OH DEAR GOD!!!!! Apparently, Tatum had sensitivity to her medications. She reacted as if she had a raging case of E Coli. If a dog has an accident in a crate, that's one thing. However, she blew with bloody, horrible, projectile, pure liquid diarrhea. And because she is a beast, not only did she get it all over her crate *and the walls between the baseboard and the walls*, she pointed her butt toward Killian and spewed foul all into his crate too. Poor Killian is pressed up against the walls of his crate crying and looking at me like why did *he* have to suffer?

Some days you're the dog, other days you're the fire hydrant. Today was a fire hydrant kind of day.

# Worst Pick Up Line Ever

I was brought up to be polite, somewhat demure, and to let silence speak louder than words. I went to the Emily Post Etiquette School at the Breakers in Palm Beach, Florida when I was 13. Now I know which fork to use, where my napkin should be at all times, and, in a nutshell, everything Barney taught Vivienne in the movie Pretty Woman.

Most people who have met me say I *look* the part of a polite woman. I have a medium build, big blue eyes, long blonde hair, and somewhat delicate features… Until I open my mouth. I curse like a truck driver for the Navy. I have a short temper, a chip on my shoulder the size of the Grand Canyon, and an ego big enough to take up the room. But I have to keep that all in check when I'm in my company car that has a Golden Retriever with the Invisible Fence ® logo on the doors and I'm wearing my work uniform.

Usually I am able to keep my mouth shut and just go about my business when I'm in line at Dunkin Donuts, or the grocery stores, or anywhere in public where people seem to forget the world does not revolve around their time table. The worst I tend to do is give people "The Look" when the child behind me in line is screaming because he can't have a candy bar or the desperate housewife who keeps talking on her cell phone while trying to place her order for double cappuccino mocha half half with melted sugar and fat free foam then getting pissy because the coffee has low fat milk, not skim because her recap of the latest nail polish for her feet was supposed to be Blushing Bride but instead it turned out more like Porky Pig couldn't be interrupted to clarify which part of her order was the least pain in the neck for the attendant behind the counter. You know who you are. Every once in a while I will mutter something under my breath or commiserate with other people in line with me who are of the same annoyed state I am.

When I'm by myself in a vehicle, like most people, I'm my own version of American Idol. Sometimes I'm Kelly Clarkson; sometimes I'm William Hung. Either way, I'm a singing and dancing fool in my car. I am in my car for 6 hours a day, I might as well enjoy my time and perhaps my representation of my company isn't as professional as it can be during those moments, but I don't care. I will belt out Disturbed, Him, Sarah McLachlan, and even an occasional Copa Cabana or Air Supply tune like my life depended on it.

It was a warm summer day and I was doing my usual thing while at a traffic light, turning the radio down and singing quieter in case someone could actually hear me and might want to put *me* out of *their* misery. I had Aurora with me and she is wistfully looking out the window as we are driving *by* the plaza where she knows there is a Dunkin Donuts and we don't appear to be turning into said plaza. Yes, my dog can actually read. There isn't a Dunkin Donuts sign or coffee shop she doesn't think is personally calling her.

As we were at the light, this guy in his jacked up, oversized Ford F-150 pick up truck pulls past me. He is your typical redneck and very proud of his backwoods status. He has the Git R Done sticker that takes up the entire back window. He's even the special individual who has a set of testicles hanging off the tow hitch. Being that it is not hunting season in August, multiple fishing rods take up the slats in his gun rack instead of muzzle-loaders or whatever guns hunters use. A car in my lane pulls forward so now I am next to the protégé of Larry the Cable Guy. I glance over toward him and he motions for me to roll my window down. Oh dear God. Being that I was in the company car I couldn't exactly say "Hell NO!" Reluctantly, I rolled down my window.

He asked, 'Hey, is that a female."

Oh dear God. "Yeah," I replied slowly.

"Is she spayed?" he asked.

"Absolutely." I replied without hesitation and possible tone of "where are you going with this?"

"Oh man. I have a male. We could have bred them," he told me.

Translation: Let's let our dogs bonk and see what happens between us. First of all: Ewwwwwww. Second of all: Ewwwwwwwww! The more I thought about it, the more insulted I became. How dare he think I would pimp out my little girl to some random doggie john at a traffic light? Then, I started wondering if that was how he tried to meet women, and I felt bad for both him and the women he met. Lastly, I felt really bad for the Bullmastiff breed if that was his criteria for screening and "testing" to continue the breed. The light eventually turned green, I went to my training appointment, and then went home to shower to wash the incident off me.

# THINGS THAT MAKE YOU GO OH DEAR GOD

There are things that make you want to throw up. For example, there is the flu, bulimia, sour milk, and half naked people in public bathrooms to name a few. Being that I am on the road all the time, I have favorite places to stop and go potty. There are certain Dunkin Donuts employees that know exactly how to make my coffee. Being that I work in New Hampshire, there are certain cows along the side of the road I stop and talk to when it's a particularly boring day.

One day, I had about fifteen minutes before an appointment. I went to one of my favorite little potty haunts. A woman walked into the bathroom before I did so proper etiquette dictates she gets first choice of any available stall. There are 2 stalls in said bathroom. A HUGE handicapped stall where a small Cessna could land and a tiny, narrow, regular stall. Well apparently, the spacious, handicapped stall was a mess as evidenced by the fact the woman walked into the stall and promptly walked back out of the stall with a look of horror and disgust on her face. If it's that gross, I don't want to use it either. She knocked on the stall door of the tiny stall and a woman answered that she would be right out. Perfect. We stood there and waited our respective turns.

Now, don't get me wrong, everyone needs love and quite honestly, I don't really care but this does play a role in the rest of the story. From the tiny stall comes a 400-pound woman. Again, I don't care what she weighs or if she had purple spots. I had to pee and the sooner we expedite it, the happier I am. The woman in front of me goes into the stall.

I will say at this juncture this particular bathroom isn't your normal, every day; you pee in the bowl, flush the toilet, and go on your merry way bathroom. This is a waterless, good for the environment, recycling toilet system and your waste is composted and recycled immediately upon exiting, shall we say. You must press the START button on the toilet; this will fill the bowl with foamy bubbles. You do your business. You then press the START button again calling for more bubbles to flush your excrement into the tank below where the composting begins. The directions are clearly posted on the walls on how to use this system. However, either the woman in front of me couldn't read or she missed the giant sign with the directions and she came bursting out within seconds of going in to the stall, visibly confused. She asked if there was water in the bowl. I recited the directions to her and she went back in to the stall and I'm assuming did her business, still confused but at least able to comprehend what she was to do next.

As I am waiting, the first, not so svelte woman faces me as she finishes washing her hands. I am about to make room at the hand dryer for her, but she proceeds to remove her shirt and put on a fresh one. Being that she was a full figured gal, I had a full frontal visual assault of cannons that were *ready to blow* pointed in my direction. That woman's 18-hour bra was clearly working overtime.

Many thoughts were running through my mind. First and foremost: Um, Ma'am? Do you not see me standing here? Second: Who does this? Don't get me wrong; I've changed my clothes while a traffic light plenty of times. I've even driven home in just my bra and panties when I've been caught in a rainstorm and hate sitting in a wet seat and I was without a change of clothes. That being said, I've never disrobed in front of a total stranger *in a public bathroom at a gas station*. I was a little nervous as to what she was going to do next because if the skirt came off next, that was just a comfort level she had that I couldn't deal with and I was going to go into the men's room and just take my chances. So I did the only thing I could think, I focused on my blackberry and typed my little heart out until the other lady came out of the stall and I ran into it and almost threw up.

# A Test of Poop Versus Patience

Aurora truly is a remarkable dog. She is balanced. She is patient. She is a dog that not only leads by example within the pack with the dogs, but within our household with the humans too. She has a quiet, subtle, yet very clear way of communicating. It was this particular incident that really made me appreciate the little life's lessons our dogs teach us and I try to remember this lesson when I am losing my mind over something trivial, and usually it's all trivial.

As I moved to be more au naturelle with the care of our dogs, I too jumped on the raw food diet for dogs bandwagon. I love the idea of raw food. There aren't any preservatives. It's actually healthier for dogs than even the high quality kibble. Dogs with chronic allergies, persistent urinary tract issues, and various gastric issues do much better on the raw food diet. Among dietary benefits, the amount of waste the dog creates is also reduced, and it is so dehydrated it crumbles into dust after a day or so upon exiting the dog.

However, with every latest and greatest new thing, there are a few downsides. The biggest downside is if you have more than one dog, especially if they are large breed dogs like mine, it can get very costly to do the raw food diet. Another drawback is there are many conflicting ideas on which raw diet and which supplements are required to give the dog a balanced meal. I researched the pros and cons of feeding the raw food diet until almost going blind one month. The bottom line is to do what feels right in your heart. Sometimes it can take a few months for the dogs' digestive tracts to adjust to the rich organ meat and high protein diet. It is called the cleansing period where the dog's body is cleansing itself of the toxins that are in commercial dog foods. Cleansing often results in some vomiting and diarrhea.

Denali couldn't tolerate the organ meat, and I don't have the patience to clean a dog and his diarrhea filled crate after a 10-hour workday every day. Call me lazy, I'm fine with it. On the other paw if you will, he could handle the chicken necks, and he and Aurora thought the chicken necks were the greatest thing since cheese. Every three weeks, I had everyone's rapt attention as I separated the necks into plastic Baggies and put them into the freezer. I had to wear non-slip shoes for fear of slipping in the pools of drool that would accumulate with every filled baggy. Tatum had a hard time with the necks and I would often come home to a soiled crate and I was told Killian was too old for the raw diet so he and Tatum stayed on their kibble diet. At the time, I was doing a combination of the chicken necks and kibble for the Mastiffs. The routine was simple; in the morning everyone got kibble and various supplements. In the evening, the Killian and Tatum got their kibble and they both drooled in envy as Mama and Doodles ate their chicken necks.

It seemed the raw food was making the mastiffs' poops very aromatic and delectable in little Tatum's nose. She had never been a poop eater before. She didn't eat poop as a puppy or even when we would go on walks she wouldn't eat the poop in which Killian had just rolled. She was a wonderful little Imp who would exfoliate your face from the million kisses she would give upon meeting you, be it for the first time or every day after work. But all of a sudden, the little beast was now hunting and eating poop. Specifically, she was eating the Mastiffs' poop.

I love my dogs until the end of time, but poop eating is a deal breaker. I found myself getting very impatient with Tatum for little things she would do in the house because I was so frustrated by what she was doing when she was outside. I tried all the conventional methods to prevent the poop eating activity. I scooped as soon as everyone pooped. I added the anti poop eating additives into everyone's food. I really don't subscribe to the sprinkle Tabasco sauce on the poop theory because really, if I'm going to go outside and be near a poop, I'm simply going to pick it up. Nothing seemed to help. I was getting very sad because I truly loved the kisses Tatum relinquished because she was so exuberant in her affection and now I didn't want her feces filled fangs anywhere near me.

One warm afternoon, I was home trying to enjoy some quiet downtime. I was in a particularly foul mood because I had just caught Tatum eating poop again and no matter how harshly I yelled at her, she kept chomping away bewildered at why I was so upset. *She* was enjoying a yummy treat, what could possibly be *my* problem? It was during the spring and there were plenty of puddles in the yard so after the Beast had her fill of poop, she washed it down with a full serving of mud puddle. She promptly came in and threw up her snack all over the living room rug.

Watered down, muddy poop was now seeping into my carpet. I was *livid*. I slammed down the television remote and screamed "TATUM" as loud as I could and started going after Tatum to chase her outside. Aurora had been on her usual perch in the love seat, she immediately bolted off the chair. She got between Tatum and I, refusing to let me go by. She would look at me and nudge my leg with her head. I knelt down next to Big Mama and she put her head into my chest then looked at me as if to say, "It is just poop. The world won't end. Now go get the carpet cleaner. It stinks in here."

It was that moment when I had a life changing epiphany.  She was right.  It *was* just poop.  No one was hurt.  Nothing was truly ruined.  If this is what I really have to worry about, I have a pretty good life and I need to start being grateful for the little things.  I pulled out the rug doctor, cleaned the carpet, apologized to Tatum for yelling at her, thanked Aurora for always being such a good teacher, then grabbed a beer to go sit on the deck and enjoyed the sounds of the outdoors.  Every once in a while when I feel myself getting worked up over something, I reflect on that moment and think, "What would Mama do?" and then call Maureen to see if she concurs.

# A WEEK OF LIFE'S LESSONS

Sometimes life is trying to teach us lessons, and it takes accidentally taking your dog's sedative to get you to wake up... Well, after you wake up that is. Wintertime is especially slow for me at work so I have plenty of time to think about what I want to do around the house for projects. It was a particular nasty three-week stretch of weather where it was either frigid out or too icy to risk taking a walk and slipping on the ice. As a result, we all had a lot of pent up energy. Even Aurora was showing signs of stir crazy because she kept trying to lift the pool table with her butt. I was bringing the dogs to daycare just to get some exercise for them and peace in the house for me.

During that time, I set my sights on the dog room. When we were building the house, we added a room that was supposed to be an office. However, the office quickly became the pets' room. Between the dog crates, ferret cage, and various food and water bowls, there wasn't room for a desk, let alone any paperwork that wouldn't get slobber on it. For as beautiful as the rest of the house is, it is very evident the dog room was an after thought that was just thrown together when we were "finishing" the house as we built it. We used the stick down tiles for flooring and after years of slobber, the tiles were peeling up. We had one lamp for light in the room that didn't match anything and the cord had been replaced numerous times because Tatum had reached out while in her crate and ate the cord. I had grown tired of the plain blue paint on the wall. I wanted to make the room fun. I wanted to make a statement. I should have had Jason, or anyone of sound mind for that matter, to be with me as I picked out the paint.

There was a misunderstanding at work the day I was picking out the paint. Dr. Zimmerman, my Plan B vet as well as sounding board when I know I'm being crazy but I'm pretty sure I have a valid point, had moved into a town that was under the jurisdiction of another Invisible Fence® independent dealer. However, her office was in the territory of my company. She had called me to tell me her dog's collar wasn't working and he was leaving the yard but her collar for her other dog was working so we were able to deduce she simply had a malfunctioning collar, a quick and easy fix. Dr. Zimmerman and I, as well as Dr. Dutton and I, have a relationship where I will in fact drop whatever I am doing to fix their Invisible Fence as quickly and as cost effectively as possible. In return, they will offer a great deal of free advice as well as give my pets priority status when there is a problem. I was able to finagle a way to fix Dr. Zimmerman's Invisible Fence® while she was at work, even though her home address belonged to another Independent Dealer.

Even though I had been given the green light to service her account, the person granting that permission didn't necessarily have that authority. I fixed her collar, finished the rest of my work for the day, and then went to Home Depot pick up supplies to add new life to the dogs' room. As a result of my actions for Dr. Zimmerman, my blackberry went off letting me know I had mail. I opened the e mail that cc:ed two of my managers and I had my butt handed to me in a group e-mail while I was standing in the paint department at Home Depot. It seems what I did was deemed to be poaching from another dealer's customer base. I was scolded like I was a three year old. I was shaking I was so mad and went back outside to my car to send the appropriate rebuttal responses for fear I might start talking *to* the blackberry as I sent my responses. I couldn't remember the last time I was that furious about anything.

However, things worked out for the best, like they usually do, Dr. Zimmerman's entire account was transferred over to our company, and I even got an apology for the misunderstanding but the damage was done. I had picked out the paint while still very, very, *very* angry. I chose Youthful Coral. If you go to www.behr.com, you can see what lovely shade of *Oh My GOD* Youthful Coral is.

Jason and I usually make a good team when it comes to painting. He cuts in along the edges and windows and I follow by painting the walls. My friend Colleen had called and I was wrapping up the conversation while he got started on the painting. He heard me coming towards the room and called out I should brace myself. I rounded the corner and then took a step backwards.

Even on just the borders around the windows, the room was yelling at me to come on in! Well I'm the genius who picked out this color; we went forward and painted the whole room. Then we did the second coat. The color was reflecting off the snow outside. With the door to the room closed, there was a glow that came from under the door that was reminiscent of the windows in the Amityville Horror movie. After a few days, we just couldn't convince ourselves this was a good choice. It was a fun color for a Caribbean hotel room. It was indeed vibrant like underwater sea life that shines so brilliantly on the Discovery Channel. It was screaming to have a Bahama Mama cocktail for breakfast. It just wasn't our style.

We decided to try to tone it down. We bought some light cream paint and fauxed over it. Now it just looked like… Well, it looked like crap. We didn't think it could go from bad to worse but it did. We didn't even bother fauxing the whole room. It was pretty obvious neither of us could look at the wall without cringing.

I even called my mother to get some decorating advice. She has impeccable taste and I thought she would be able to help. She was less than supportive of the original choice. She used the word "vomit" a great deal. I was even told a dog of Aurora's stature deserved to be surrounded by calming colors, not ones that make her want to vomit. Case and point why I am the way I am, every decision needs to be based on the dogs' perceived comfort level as dictated by my mother.

We decided to start over and work from the bottom up. We pooled the Home Depot and Lowe's Gift cards we had received at Christmas. We got a great deal on some earth toned porcelain tile. We painted the bottom half of the room a dark taupe, the top half a rich, warm cream color, and found a vintage border that showed various dog breeds in classic picture frames that combined the two tones we had chosen that we placed in the middle of the room. We installed recessed lighting. As we transformed the room from run down blah, to over ripened mango turned vomit, into the doggie sanctuary, we found we were calmed by the colors. The moral here is: Don't pick out paint when you're angry.

The sense of calm didn't last very long. Well, sort of but not really in a good way. As we were patting ourselves on the back for creating such a nice room for the dogs two nights later, Porter walked by Tatum who was lying by the warmth of the pellet stove. Tatum cried in pain. It was a little odd, so I went to sit by her to see if there were any obvious signs that would make her cry. When I rubbed her belly, she yiped in pain. I went to the kitchen to see if I could find something to take the edge off the pain for her. My plan was to give her an aspirin or something and if she was still crying in pain the next morning, I would call to make an appointment for her.

I found one of Porter's sedatives from when he was undergoing his Mange treatments and got as far as taking it out of the bottle and setting it on the stove. Jason got up and was palpating Tatum all over and really making her cry in pain. I snapped at him to stop it; she was in pain; stop making it worse. As I was opening the refrigerator door for a piece of cheese, Jason called out her belly was hard and she was really screaming when he pressed on it. Since that was a symptom of a possible gastric torsion, or bloat, which is 100% fatal if untreated, I fired up the truck, wrapped her in her jacket and off we went to the ER. She cried the whole way and was shaking in pain. That commute was by far the longest 15 minutes of our lives.

We were seen quickly and while she was still shaking and whimpering, she seemed to calm down while on the exam table. The doctor requested we put her on the floor so she could do a more thorough exam. Tatum circled the floor a few times then squatted and let out the biggest pee I've ever seen and she seemed to feel 100% better immediately after emptying a gallon of urine on the floor. My mood shifted from sheer terror to pure annoyance. I had let the dogs out to pee just an hour before we went to the ER.

However, just to be sure, the doctor suggested a couple x rays just to be sure everything else seemed fine. The x ray showed a slow emptying of her food that was still in her stomach. A dose of Pepcid and time were prescribed, the typical take two of these and call me in the morning. At a subsequent visit to another physician months later for a totally unrelated issue, she voiced whether Tatum had a crystal plug blocking her urethra and perhaps even though I had let everyone out for potty earlier that evening, she was physically unable to go and the constant palpations forced enough pressure to dislodge the plug and she was able to release the urine and make the pain of an overfilled bladder go away. It made sense.

But getting back to the next morning, I was rushing around and getting everyone ready for a day in their crates and getting myself ready for work. Tatum seemed no worse for the wear. As I was making the dogs' breakfast, I looked down on the stove and saw what I thought was my daily folic acid tablet. I popped the tablet and continued getting everyone ready.

About a half hour later, as I'm driving down the road for the first of my three appointments for that day, I realized what I did. I had taken Porter's sedative. I went to my first call, and for the most part, felt fine. Maybe a smidge off, but fine none the less. However, to be safe, I called my doctor's office just in case there is a toxic reaction to Acepromazine in humans. They had no record of Acepromazine for humans but Promazine was taken off the market, no mention as to why. I was told to call my vet.

Oh sure, add fire to that raging inferno. While they truly love me for the neurotic nut that I am, even they don't think I should be in public unsupervised some days. Today was clearly one of them. After the initial laughter subsided, the doctor told me that Acepromazine was a pretty powerful sedative, and in an effort to cover his liability, if I felt the need to nap, I should do so in the emergency room to make sure my vitals could be monitored by trained professionals. I decided I would see how I felt after my second call and go from there.

After finishing the second call, I was exhausted. I was thinking clearly, but man was I tired. I had one more call to do. It was supposed to be a simple system check. A call I can normally do in fifteen minutes, and it was blessedly in the same direction as my house. I stopped for a cup of coffee and to use the bathroom at Dunkin Donuts before going to my call. I looked in the mirror and could barely make out the blueness in my eyes. I resorted to the face I used to make when I would go home after partying and thought my parents couldn't tell I was stoned. God I looked goofy. And I'm pretty sure they knew.

Finally, I made it home. My couch never looked so comfy. I checked the answering machine and there were three messages from my doctor's office, each call had a greater sense of worry in the nurse's voice. Apparently, I neglected to mention I was on my cell phone when I called. I called them back and assured them I was fine, but really wanted to take a nap. I was told after they had done extensive research, they weren't able to find much information on Acepromazine in humans, and before they recommended I take my much-needed nap, I was told I needed to call Poison Control. It had been seven hours since I took the pill, I was sure I would be fine at this point, but protocol is protocol. I called Poison control. At this point, I was beginning to feel I was going to end up calling everyone who could and would call me an idiot for taking dog medication.

I was grateful that I wasn't actually laughed at when I called the nice folks at Poison Control. In fact, four people a week take their pets' medications. Really? I wasn't sure if I should take comfort in the fact I'm not the only moron out there or be disheartened because there are so many of us. I was allowed to take a nap and I should feel fine in the morning. Yay. I e mailed Dr. Dutton just to let him know in case one of his clients makes a similar mistake, and off to Snooze Ville I went. Or tried to anyway. First, my doctor's office called back. They wanted to be sure Poison Control said I would be fine. I have to admit, I felt relieved to know they cared so much. Grateful even. Then, my mother called. Just to say hi.

"Hello," I said, barely audible.

"Are you sick?" she asked.

"No, just napping. What's up?"

"But you're not sick?"

"No. I accidentally took Porter's medication. I'm just very tired. What's up?"

"Why do you keep your pet's meds and yours in the same place?" I admit, it is a valid question, one that I had now been asked at least

3 times, and I can't even counter with I'm not that stupid because clearly, I am.

"I don't. It's a long story. What's up?"

"You are doing your best to kill your liver aren't you?"

"Yeah, that's it. *What do you want?*"

We chatted and at that point, I gave up on the nap. Jason came home shortly thereafter. I was starving. Very little has an affect on my appetite, heavy sedatives included. He made dinner, and we hung out on the couch. I tried to stay awake as long as possible. I made it to 8:30 and climbed into bed. That was the BEST night's sleep I have had in a while. A couple days later I took out the Acepromazine and the Folic Acid tablet. They look pretty darn close to the same. But the message was received; slow down, and put things away when you are done with them. And don't pick out paint when you're angry.

# Your Dogs

By all accounts, the dogs are mine. Never, in our entire marriage, or relationship for that matter, has Jason ever brought home a pet or even contemplated the idea of adding a new member to our family. There was 3 months I thought I wanted to be a mother of an actual child. That passed. And even then, it was still my decision when I wanted to be a mother. Then it was my decision that, well; I really don't like children. My cousin, Joelle, has the most perfect children; incredibly respectful and well behaved, and just the biggest love bugs ever. My other cousins, Allen and Michael, are also wonderful children who demonstrate the same level of sweetness and respect. If you could promise me a Jake, Jesse, Julia, Allen or Michael, then I would actually consider being a mother. But you can't. So I won't have a child. The world is probably a better place because of it. But even for you parents of two legged children, you know it's never a good sign when you come home after a long day of work and your spouse refers to the offspring as *yours*.

Bless Jason's heart, he tries so hard to not take it hard that he knows he pales in comparison to how the dogs feel about me. If he gets up to let them out in the morning on a day we both have off from work, he has to really coax them to get up and leave me to answer their respective calls of nature. He then stays downstairs to make coffee but they all come bombing back upstairs to snuggle with me. He usually has to shoo away at least two dogs from his spot in the bed upon his return upstairs.

When I have an early morning or a late night at work, he feeds them. If I can't take them to the vet's or daycare or some other appointment, he will go to work late or leave his job early to bring them. He really does love the dogs like I do and would do anything he could to take care of them, but they love me best. He is equally as protective of them as I am, tries to deflect fools from sticking their hands in our vehicles because he doesn't want our dogs to be in a bad position, not because he cares about some dim-witted individual that lacks appropriate dog knowledge. He used to tell me to bring the dogs to the vet if it would make me feel better. Now he's the one urging me to bring them in, just in case it could be something. I've made him into the monster he's become too.

In his defense of why the dogs like me better, I'm home more than he is. Even if we are home together, Jason usually has some project that he is working on and I'm usually slacking off playing on the computer. The dogs are used to coming to me for everything and they are used to me giving them most of everything they want or need. I typically feed them every day. I am usually home longer in the morning and the first to arrive in the afternoon so I typically let them out for the potties. I train them. I walk them. And I have a much better read on them and know how to direct them into what I want them to do based on their body language.

Being a dog trainer in New Hampshire in the winter doesn't exactly have a high demand. In some ways, my job is like that of being in school and my days will be canceled due to inclement weather. And just like when we were all 8 years old, when I received the news that work had been called off due to snow, I would run around the house doing the dance of joy and then jump back in to bed and go to sleep til 10:00. Reruns of ER started at 10:00, so then we all snuggled on the couch seeing if Dr. Carter would care too much and how much of a jerk Dr. Romano could be to some poor, unsuspecting resident. Seriously, I *love* my job.

The first winter I worked for the Canine Fence Company was brutal in terms of snowfall. We received what seemed like a foot of snow every fifteen minutes so I truly did not leave my house for six weeks to go to work. Then I broke my wrist. It was innocent enough. I have a lot of pent up energy and, since I deal with the general public on a daily basis, anger at the ignorance of how people raise their dogs flows through me like the Star Wars Force. The music I like doesn't quell that anger either. I am into the music of Disturbed, Nickleback, Trapt, and Kiss has always been my favorite group. Their lyrics don't exactly invoke romance and roses and the betterment of mankind.

For Christmas that year, Santa brought me a punching bag. I loved it! It was one of the best presents that didn't have diamonds in it. After my uncle passed away when he deserved to live so much longer, I went to town on my punching bag. At the funeral, my hands were bruised and scraped from the intense beating I gave my punching bag. It truly was one of the best therapy sessions I have ever had that didn't involve a discussion.

I didn't have any work one day so I was squaring off with my punching bag. I cued up my Anger Management CD and was really getting into my work out. I wasn't six minutes into it when I extended my palm to nail the bag on its swing back return when all of a sudden I was dropped to my knees, screaming in pain. Oh dear God this hurt and there was now a lump on my wrist that wasn't there just fifteen seconds prior. Being that I was in the basement, I crawled on my good hand and both knees to the stairs. At the top of the stairs were two very concerned canines. At the time, we only had Killian and Aurora. They couldn't break through the barrier to get downstairs but they knew their Momma was in trouble.

I got upstairs and called Jason. He said I should ice it and see how I felt later. Clearly, in between my sobs, he didn't understand the excruciating pain I was in. I called my Aunt Donna. She left work and brought me to the ER. As it turned out, I was now in the same room that many of my family members had shared. My uncle had been in there for a shoulder injury. My aunt was in there when her appendix ruptured. My cousin was in there with a severe case of bronchitis. Now I was in there with a broken wrist. The way we could tell it was the same room was the same blood splatter had been on the wall in the exact same place for every family member.

After the radiologist had taken the x rays and brought me back to what was now known as the Patnode Suite, my uncle showed up since he was down the street at a dentist appointment when my aunt called to say we were at the hospital. It was just another one of many family reunions in the ER. Then, the attending radiologist, who happened to be their neighbor stopped in to say hi and that he saw the x ray. I asked if my wrist was broken. He said, while nodding his head, that he didn't know and the doctor was reviewing the film and we needed to wait for the doctor. I recognized his voice.

When I was in the radiology room, immediately following the x ray that was taken fifteen minutes prior to officially meeting the neighbor, Mark, I saw a picture of a wrist on a screen through that little window in the room the radiologist hides behind, and I heard a voice say, "Oh, that can't be good." That voice was Mark, my Aunt and Uncle's neighbor. My wrist was definitely broken.

The doctor came in shortly after and explained there was a fracture but due to the swelling, they weren't able to cast my wrist today. He produced a huge splint and told me to take off my sweatshirt so he could splint my arm. I was reluctant to remove my sweatshirt. Not because I'm shy and had half my family in the curtain area with me. I said, "You're all going to laugh at me." My uncle, thinking I wanted privacy, started to leave the area as I removed my sweatshirt.

I was wearing my Super Girl sports bra and somehow the fact I was now broken seemed comical.

Per the doctor's instructions, I was not allowed to search for elusive wire breaks with a cast on my wrist. Oh pity. You mean I couldn't try to chisel at the frozen tundra and freeze my butt off trying to fix a break in the wire that an over zealous plow guy created? For six whole weeks? Really? I was in Heaven. I spent that winter barely leaving my couch all the while getting paid. During that time, we adopted Denali. This was the first time in his life Denali had been shown love and he defended that source of love with ferocity unrivaled by any dog I have ever met. I was home with my dogs 24-7 for six weeks. If, for some unforeseen reason, they weren't my dogs before, they were now.

However, all good things must come to an end. I couldn't break my wrist every winter without arousing suspicion, and once the snow melts, my siren of work calls me. With the springtime come the open floodgates of training and service calls for everyone who had been waiting for the snow to melt for me to now pursue. It is not uncommon for me to leave the house at 7:00 AM and get home at 7:00 PM during April and May. I may be tired, but I don't complain much since I spent the last three months on my keister. I truly love what I do, and every two weeks, my checkbook shows the rewards of my hard work.

When I'm home for those twelve weeks in the winter, I have three furry shadows. I don't go to the bathroom by myself. I don't fold laundry alone. Porter makes sure all the dishes are "clean" before I close the dishwasher door. When I feed the wood stove that's in the basement, there are three faces at the top of the stairs wondering when I will reappear in their line of vision. Aurora is busy holding down the love seat in case it should try to float away. I have guard dogs. They guard me. What can I say?

On the other hand, when Jason's home and I'm not, whether he is working in the house, the basement, or outside, they all retire to the living room and spend the day on their respective couches or beds. They don't follow him. They don't "help" him. They basically wait for me to get home by sleeping away the day. Even if Jason feeds them breakfast and dinner, takes them for a ride, or even walks them, they aren't velcroed to his behind like they are to mine.

It was one of those particularly long days that Jason was home on a Saturday and he didn't have a good day with the dogs. This evening, I came home after a long twelve-hour day at work. The lights were all out in the house except in the bathroom in our bedroom. The dogs were in their crates. It was very quiet. As a general rule, Jason likes to let the dogs out to greet me when I get home because, as the melee ensues of barking and howling, "Mom's HOME!" he lets them bomb outside to greet me. Usually, unless a really good rerun episode of Law and Order is on, I do the same. Since no one was welcoming me with open slobbers, I went inside. I tentatively went upstairs and heard Jason was in the shower.

"Hi Honey, how was your day?" I asked.

"**_You_** have four very bad, bad dogs." Oh, that's never good.

"What happened?" I asked.

"Well, Aurora jumped up on the counter and ate my sandwich box. Porter pooped on the floor in front of the bathroom downstairs and smeared poop all over the tile. Tatum ate the poop but didn't do a good job of cleaning where it had smeared. And Killian, *your* Christ Dog, threw up what looks like the remains of someone's bedding in Tatum's crate. Banner day. Just a red letter, banner day."

Yup. Those are *my* dogs. There's just never a dull moment around here,

# TEN YEAR ANNIVERSARY

It was our ten-year wedding anniversary. Like any couple, married or not, with or without children, ten years is a long time to be with someone and still actually like them. Jason and I had a four year courtship prior to the nuptials so that's even longer to still like someone. Let's face it, who we are when we are in our twenties filled with visions of romance, roses, and all the happy carefree choices is vastly different from who we are in our thirties when we have such things as mortgages and taxes versus rent, car payments of an actually nice car and not the used beater we found at Ed's Garage and Taxidermy, grocery bills take the place of bar tabs, and well, I'm a *heck* of a lot more tired than when I was 25. I'm not looking forward to my 40's. Like any relationship, we had some really, really, really good times and some really, really, really, rotten times. However, nothing worth having comes easy and when it got bad, we stood at the crossroads and opted to fight for what we had been creating since we were teenagers. It paid off.

We decided to celebrate our anniversary in Aruba, where we spent our honeymoon. We've made a couple extra trips in between because oh my, Aruba is such a paradise on earth. The beaches are gorgeous. The people are so friendly. The shopping is abundant. And the bar opens at 11 in the morning. One year we had quite possibly the worst vacation in that if it could go wrong, it did. It started with missing our connecting flights, we lost our luggage, *of course,* and it was just a comedy of what else can go wrong? But we were in Aruba. *Nothing* can be that bad.

One of the appeals of leaving the country for a vacation is *no one can contact us.* Whatever the emergency may be will just have to wait because we are on vacation. We go on vacation to truly disconnect. I pour my heart and soul into my job and with the blackberry I make myself available to my clients 24 hours, seven days a week, even during football season, should they have questions or concerns. However, when I'm on vacation, for those seven days, other people's problems are no longer my concern.

Another group I disconnect from is my coworkers. I go on vacation to get away from work, not take it with me. That's not to say I don't love my colleagues or that I don't adore the people whose lives I touch every day, but I do need some me time. We also don't go on vacation to meet new people. Sure, we will talk to people we meet, but we aren't the type to exchange e mails and keep in touch. Jason works in retail, I deal with the public in their homes. We need that week to unwind and recharge.

The flip side is we can't contact anyone either. Usually about three weeks before leaving, my stress level starts gradually increasing to the point I just about snap at the thought of leaving my dogs and not being able to be reached in the event of an emergency. The sane side of me, yes, there really is one, knows between connecting flights etc. there isn't a hope in Hades of me being able to do anything if a problem arises because it is about 10 hours between getting into the cab from the resort to the airport and getting home. Or, in the case of our trip home this year, we left Aruba at noon and got home at 2:30 the following morning due to bad weather and delayed flights. So yes, I am very aware if a situation presented itself, I would be helpless to fix it. However, being the control freak that I am, it terrifies me to the core that something could happen to one of them and I wouldn't be there to use what little knowledge I had gained while being a veterinary technician to make decisions. That knowledge has come in handy on more than one occasion and actually saved Denali's life from an already premature death.

He had not kept any food down for two weeks, but his attitude and appetite remained good so I did the bland diet and Pepto route. After coming home for the second week in a row to a puke filled crate and this time he wasn't keeping water down, and Jason was out of town again, I brought Denali to the emergency room.

I was sent home with a diagnosis of congestive heart failure and no concrete explanation of the acute onset of vomiting. For three days, I was a mess. I knew the day was supposed to come, but he seemed so vibrant and healthy otherwise. Jason would call to check in and I wouldn't be able to speak because I was so upset. Then, three days later, the fog of sadness lifted and I started thinking. I had seen the x rays of his chest, no real fluid in the lungs to speak of. Denali wasn't coughing and he didn't sound wet when he would breathe. And he didn't have any real fluid build up elsewhere in his body. By no means whatsoever am I a vet, but I do not need letters after my name to know those are not the hallmarks of congestive heart failure.

I was *all over* Dr. Dutton with phone calls and incessant e mails to make sure this diagnosis of a death sentence was correct. It wasn't. Denali had an upset stomach due the fact I had been trying to switch him over to the raw food diet and the organ meat was too rich for him. Jason was still out of town when the accurate diagnosis was revealed and to be sure, there was no containing the sheer venom I was spewing. Potty words were flying to describe the potty words I was using to illustrate my rage. People make mistakes, and if this were someone else's dog, I would try to comfort my friend with the "Doctors are human too." But this was *my dog* and if I permit you to treat my dog, yes, I said it; you had better know what you are talking about. Hell hath no fury like me. By the way, that particular doctor at the emergency room and I have mutually agreed that his services will never again be provided for my dogs. And that is just fine.

I digress. We dropped Tatum Belle, Porter, and Killian off at the Brookwood Pet Resort, and Big Mama stayed with my mom. To add to my stress level, Aurora developed a bladder infection the day before we left. However, even I will admit a UTI isn't the end of the world. I added the antibiotics to the pre bagged food I sent with her with to my mother's house and had no doubts everything would be fine. I had filled the baggies of their food labeled and dated for breakfast and dinner.

I had drawn up lists of emergency contacts. And Maureen was going to call mid week just to check on everyone. They were going to be fine. Upon dropping the three stooges off, Tatum was in the lobby, sitting perfectly, absolutely shouting to everyone she was there and she was ready to claim her throne. Porter fed into the excitement and he too, announced he was there and would also be a force with which to reckon. Killian, well, he was barking, but I don't think he knew why. They were going to be fine. Upon dropping Aurora off at my mom's, her dog, Brinkley, immediately started chewing on Aurora and mounting her. Aurora gave me a look that said "I'm going to handle this if you don't," and within 30 seconds, she nailed Brinkley with a "I could knock you into next week and if you keep it up, I just might," snap of the teeth and swing of her head. She was going to be fine.

The next morning at 3:30, we were up and ready to head to paradise. Our flight was uneventful, our luggage arrived, and the taxi ride to the hotel was short. We unpacked, put on a shield of sun block, dressed in our bathing suits, and off to the bar we went. As a general rule, we spend the first day just sipping fruity drinks and watching the waves roll across the ocean then soak up the breath taking sunset.

Being that we were up at Oh God Thirty that morning, shortly after the sunset we were yawning. We grabbed a nightcap and headed off to our hotel room. Aruba truly is a very safe island. There are no precautions about leaving the resort. In fact, it's encouraged to go downtown, either via a cab or you can even take the city bus. The motto of the country is "One Happy Island," and it sincerely is.

That being said, as we were on the balcony enjoying the night air, I looked down and there was a man standing just on the inside of the lights from the hotel, and he was masturbating. I cried out "Oh dear God," and went into the hotel room. It was a guest for sure, and there were security personnel walking up and down the boardwalk just inches from where this pervert was standing but it just set the tone for creep show and for the rest of the trip, we never saw the Prince of Self Pleasure again, but Jason didn't let me out of his sight either.

Over the next few days, we made the observation that we, as Americans, were the minority. It wasn't that people weren't speaking English. It was the British and Dutch accents in which they spoke that tipped us off that Europe was on holiday. The other big, and I mean that in every sense of the word, big clue was that everywhere you looked, there were exposed breasts. Apparently, topless sunbathing is the norm in Europe and we were in every teenage boy's utopia. That being said, not everyone should be exposed to everyone's exposure. Holy Christmas there was some scary looking mammeries. Yeah yeah yeah everyone is beautiful, blah blah blah. I'm no Pamela Anderson myself. However, when everything is pointing toward your knees, put a top on. There were even a few people who let us know, in no uncertain terms that the "twins" were bought and paid for as the scars were still evident. Being that my 40th birthday isn't too far from the horizon, I have even entertained keeping the girls perky through augmentation. But just for the record, I would plan to keep the scars hidden so as to not let everyone know just how vain I am.

We had such a lazy, relaxing week. I burned through three and a half novels. We did our usual snorkel tour as well as rent a car to go to our favorite haunt of Baby Beach. We napped. We played in the water. We had our much needed *vacation.* On our actual anniversary, we had a Spa by the Sea. We signed up for an hour massage that was in a hidden little cove that was peaceful enough no one bothered you as they walked by but close enough to the ocean that you heard every wave as is descended upon the shore. What could be better?

I had been dealing well with being away from the dogs all week. I missed them terribly, but at the root of everything, I also needed a break from them. Jason and I play a little game where I ask him what the kids are doing and he makes up these crazy activities to make it sound like they too are having a vacation filled with fun and frolic. It's crazy, but it works. The massage would further distract me from being away from my four legged shadows. Our massage was scheduled for 11:00 and we needed to be there at 10:45 to fill out the paperwork. We used the free time after breakfast to sit under an umbrella and read our books.

From out of nowhere, a bird lands under my beach chair. It wasn't as much of a landing as it was more of a thud into the sand. I looked and this little bird, about the size of a parakeet, was clearly in distress. He was breathing heavily, he couldn't fly, and he could barely jump away when I reached down for him. Birds don't show distress until they are gravely ill and this poor guy was circling the drain. As sad as it made me, nature was going to take its course. I went to the kitchen, asked for a pair of gloves because I sure didn't want whatever was ailing him, and gently took the bird and placed him under a bush. Then I went to the snack bar and got a small piece of bread to give to the little guy knowing he was never going to eat it. Upon my return, another bird was mauling the crap out of the sick bird, giving a new window into genocide. It was a sight of evil and natural selection all at once. There was a look of pure malice on the other birds face as he was smothering the sick bird to death. It sickened me. However, in the back of my mind, the theme from the Lion King, Circle of Life, played through my mind, and Jason and I lightly joked about it.

It seemed to me that was one rotten omen and the wheels in my mind were racing. I lasted about 5 minutes before I bought an international calling card and called Maureen. As luck would have it, she had called Brookwood for me about an hour prior and everyone was fine. Tatum, she reported, was being an angel as per the staff of Brookwood. I questioned if she had inquired about the correct dog. She said she asked the same thing. I opted not to call my mother because, well, being scolded for being paranoid while I'm in a fragile state has never really helped my frame of mind. I was relieved about the three stooges and was going to be able to enjoy my massage.

On my way back to the beach chair, I peeked to see Petey, I named the little bird Petey, no one should die without a name, had passed away. As irony would have it, I placed him under the bush that served as the entranceway for the restaurant we were having dinner that night. Something told me that was still not a good sign, but what was I going to do? Move a now dead bird elsewhere? I let him rest where he was to serve as iguana food and again, quietly sang the Lion King theme song to myself.

All is well that ends well. On our last day, we had to check out and head to the airport at noon. We strategically planned breakfast, packing, lunch, and since the bar opened at 11, we planned to suck back as many of those free drinks as we could in an hour's time. We enjoyed an uneventful flight to Dulles International airport where we were scheduled for a two-hour layover. Jason was now reading one of the books I had read and I was reading one of the books he had read so we would stop and compare notes every once in a while.

Upon landing, he pulled out his blackberry and asked if he dared turning it on. Ohhhhhh. The peril of doing that is we were still on vacation and if you respond to one e mail, it could create a flurry of other e mails. We made a pact. We would read all the e mails but not respond to one e mail. I had 36 e mails. He had 168. I started quoting Will Farrell from the movie, Anchor Man. "People 'know' you. You're kind of a big deal. You also have many leather bound books." He thwapped me with his blackberry. I also turned on my cell phone and called my mother to check on Big Mama. My mother assured me she was fine and as we chatted I noticed our flight was delayed an hour.

To be clear, my mother is not Carol Brady, Cindy Walsh, or Hannah Montana's mother. I never came home from school to smell brownies baking in the oven. And if I was having some sort of emotional crisis, you can be assured I was told to suck it up. When I was ten years old, I fell off a swing at recess and was unconscious due to a concussion. I had to go to school the next day because if I could walk *to the bathroom*, I wasn't sick.

That being said, she is still a mother who needs to know her child is safe and will stress, in her own way, until she knows I am safe. So is she warm and fuzzy? No. But she does have mother bear instincts, as one operating room nurse found out the hard way when the doctor ordered an antibiotic that is a cousin of penicillin twice removed through divorce and death. A ferret had bit me and lacerated my nerve and it required surgery to repair it. I go into anaphylactic shock if I take penicillin and my mother stood over me and demanded the nurse get the doctor to prescribe a new antibiotic and I wasn't going into that operating room until my *mom* was satisfied with the drugs of choice. In many respects, it's fair to say *I'm* the monster *she* created.

At the news of my delayed flight, she instructed me to call with updates basically until my butt was secured to my seat, my seatbelt was fastened tightly and my seat and tray table were in the upright and locked position. Part of her concern was for me, however the other issue was she had brought Aurora home for me an hour prior so I wouldn't have to make a million trips all over creation to pick up the dogs when we got home. If we were going to be stranded in Washington, she wanted to make sure Big Mama was going to be all right.

As it turned out, our flight was delayed for almost three hours. Mom didn't need to go back to our house. We went to the bar. It was Game Two of the NBA Finals, Celtics versus the Lakers. I was remotely interested, being from New Hampshire, Go Home Team Go, but not so much that after a few beers we didn't mind relinquishing our seats so that others may enjoy the game. I got up from our table to pay the tab leaving Jason at the table, a mere eight feet away, if that, to finish his beer. Jason has commented on several occasions that he does not know anyone who total strangers approach on a regular basis like they do to me. Anyone who knows me also knows that as a general rule, the vibe I send out isn't "Let's be friends." It often tends to be "Get away from me and leave me alone." As I was reaching for the credit card slip to sign, a patron sitting at the bar asked me if I wanted to see a magic trick. I was too tired to be a Smartass. Oh why not, I replied "sure."

He takes the slip I am supposed to sign, writes something on it, and then tells me to say a number between one and ten.

"Eight," I said.

"Divide that in half," he instructed.

"Four," I answered.

"Now subtract one," he said.

"What is this, math class?" I thought. "Three," I sighed.

"Now add that number and your previous answer together."

"Seven," I replied, this time not hiding much of the 'what is your point?' tone in my voice.

He beamed with pride, flipped over the piece of paper and showed me he had written the number seven. Oh dear God, *that's* his magic trick? Simple math? Please, oh for the love of all that is holy, **please** tell me this isn't this guy's pick up line. I was as irritated as he was proud of himself. I took my receipt, signed it, and pushed it way down the bar as far as I could away from him and hissed, "Have a nice flight." I turned around to Jason and mouthed, "finish your beer now" and said out loud "And get me my Bullmastiff."

I truly feel, in my heart of hearts, that if I were threatened, my dogs would in fact rise to the occasion and protect me. Now, being that I had spent the last week reading various Dean Koontz novels and delving into the world of fiction where human nature is at its worst yet the events in the books are known to make the evening news, *by no means* am I tempting any psycho serial killers to come test my theory. However, that sense of well being that comes with a 300 pound security system with teeth makes me feel very vulnerable when it's not at my backside, or on the loveseat.

# AN UNEXPECTED GOODBYE

It had been a crap week. What makes me so sad about that week was I had an amazing massage and was feeling all Zen the week prior. Thank you Jen. Nothing was bothering me. I was able to find the positive in everything. Long drives to my first and last appointments? It's fine. I was getting paid for drive time. Moronic customers whose dogs were smarter than them? The trainings went that much faster. Sometimes, life just boils down to no matter what's going on, always try and find the positive.

But after a while, when the crap seems to keep rolling down the hill you are standing at the base of, your shoes get dirty and it pisses you off. It started on a Sunday. We were at the lake with my Dad and friends and we were all having a good time. Good food. Good drinks. Good conversation. Beautiful weather. We had Tatum and Killian with us and they were being very good. Tatum was so happy to see everybody she was wagging her tail so hard into the walls on the boat that it started bleeding and she was then thwapping that happy bloody tail of hers all over everyone and everything making everything a bloody mess. Around 5:00, we noticed Tatum had some bug bite bumps. Around 6:00, she had several bug bite bumps. By 7:00, the number of hives that were covering her body was increasing at an exponential rate. We decided to leave the lake and get her home and get some Benadryl in her system.

Naturally, on the way home I called Maureen to discuss the latest malady to befall one of the dogs. She also suffers from chronic hives so I knew she would tell me if Tatum would be fine on Benadryl or of a trip to the ER was warranted. She agreed to try the Benadryl but if she got worse, we should take her to the ER. We were about half way home when I turned on the light to actually check on poor Tatum because her head felt like a mountain range of hives had developed across her forehead. Her eyes were swelling shut and her muzzle was so swollen she no longer looked like a Pit Bull but a Boxer. I called the ER and it just so happened Dr. Dutton was covering a shift there. That was all the green light I needed, we were bringing the littlest beast to the Emergency Room.

We arrived at the ER around 8:30. Oh Dear Lord. She looked *awful!* She was covered from her nose to her toes in hives. Her eyes were mere slits. The hole in my stomach was growing by the nanosecond with panic. Dr. Dutton came into the exam room and calmed me down with a quick resolution to Tatum's situation. We were to leave her for the night and they would treat her intravenously with Benadryl and steroids to knock the swelling down. Being that her reaction fell in the moderate to severe column, he felt she might need a second dose of medication at 1:00 AM and I could pick her up the following morning on my way to work. It was a plan I could live with. He even promised she could sleep with him while he dozed between emergencies. I warned him she was a bed hog that like to sleep nose to toes and often kicked.

I felt better that she was going to live to bark about it. That being said, I have only left my dogs to be hospitalized twice. The first was when Tatum was spayed and I wanted to sleep in late the following morning and the second was when Aurora had her Acruciate ligament repaired and she wouldn't have to do stairs for potty by letting her stay overnight at the hospital. At the time, Audra, one of the best veterinary technicians I've met, was working until 10:00 PM so she would call me if there were a problem. However, for everyone else's surgeries, including the recent hip surgery Killian had the previous month, or surgeries for the intestinal obstructions Tatum and Killian had, I always brought them home with me so I could closely monitor them myself through the night. I knew that Tatum was in excellent hands, and being that she was already so pathetic, I knew she would get extra love and attention.

Monday morning came and I picked up Tatum. She was doing well, 90% of the swelling had dissipated, and I was sent home with 2 doses of Prednisone to further the swelling and itch control. A common side effect of Prednisone, or any steroid for that matter, is increased drinking which leads to increased peeing. I was able to bring her home to let her rest and go back to work. Guess what I came home to that afternoon? A potty filled crate and urine soaked dog. It was Porter's first day of obedience class that started in an hour and I still had to feed everyone and take Porter for a quick walk to release some pent up energy before going to class to help him focus better.

I was able to basically throw the crate liner outside, get everyone fed, and fly out the door with Porter to take him for a quick walk before his class. We made it to his class and I spent the next hour gloating at how well our little boy did because he already had a handle on many skills. We were simply honing those skills to help boost his confidence and reign in what was becoming teenage sass as he was now a year and a half old and dogs do go through their own version of Terrible Twos.

As we were leaving the parking lot to go home, we saw a dog running down the road. It was now 8:35 at night and while the road isn't crazy with traffic, it's dark out and she's a Chocolate Labrador. By the time someone would see her, she would be under the tires. We stopped the car, managed to catch her, and realize the tags she was wearing were of minimal use to us: her Rabies Tag and her town license tag. Those aren't going to help me find her owners at that hour. So we knocked on a couple doors of the houses that were nearby to see if anyone owned her. No one did. I called the Animal Control officer and was told he was busy at the moment, but could be there in a half hour. While I wasn't thrilled at the thought of sitting outside my car for a half hour with this dog, I wasn't about to let her get killed either.

After an hour of sitting outside the car, I called the police department back to get an update on the estimated time of arrival for the officer. The man on the phone was polite but basically told me he will get there when he gets there, a dog on the side of the road isn't exactly an urgent event for the police department at that moment in time. He did tell me if I felt I needed to go, he would understand. If I felt I needed to go? And do what? Let her go? No, I'll keep waiting, but let's go; I'm getting cold. My attire for the evening was shorts, a sweatshirt, and my Teva sandals.

At the hour and a half mark of still no officer, I called back. Now I'm just going to be a pain in the behind until someone comes to protect and serve this dog. Again, I was told he appreciates me waiting, but this still didn't constitute an emergency in the world of crime management. However, this time I was told the officer was en route and I could expect him within 15 minutes.

Thirty minutes later, the officer arrives in his regular squad car. The first words out of his mouth are, "I can't take her in this car. Can't you just take her? If I take her, I'm only going to be able to put her in a crate for the night."

Are you kidding me? Jason and I just spent two hours sitting on the side of the road for you to come out here and not have the appropriate vehicle and then have the audacity to ask us to take this dog ourselves?!? Gee, why didn't we think to do that? I had more than tone in my voice when I mentioned we had four dogs, one of whom was already IN my car, and no, we weren't taking her and I wasn't about to let her run the streets all night. So the officer and I go back and forth a couple times and he says he has to go back to the station to get the appropriate vehicle in which to transport the dog to the shelter where she'll have to stay for the night. Oh, for the love of all that is holy, how long is this going to take I asked. He said he would be back within a half hour. I snarled for him to hurry back. He ended up coming back within five minutes because apparently, he was wearing his super secret decoder ring that gave him special powers to put the dog in the back of his regular squad car and bring the dog to the holding facility for stray dogs. However, said Wonder Twin ring bearer didn't have the foresight to bring a leash so he took mine. Schmuck. We got home at 11:15 and went to bed.

Let no good deed go unpunished. I woke up Tuesday and was peeing blood. Normally, I will just go to the ER, pay the $100 co-pay and get those six magic pills of Cipro antibiotic that make all urinary tract infections and the agony that accompanies them go away. For those of you who have never had a UTI, they are God's way of letting you know you have angered him somehow. It feels like you have to go potty every 10 minutes and when you do, it feels like someone is standing on your bladder and that person is wearing sandpaper shoes. When I worked for Dr. Dutton, any time an owner called saying their pet was urinating blood, I made an extra effort to squeeze that pet in because I was beyond empathetic when it came to a UTI.

However, after my previous UTI, I had the foresight to get the over the counter medication that is supposed to help with the symptoms for when the next infection occurred. I took the medication and set out to go get myself a gallon of cranberry juice. On my way to the store, I got a call from Jason. He had run out of gas on his way to work. Good Lord what was wrong with the universe? Why were we being punished? I found him on the side of the road, got him back to his motorcycle, and continued on my regular mission of finding cranberry juice.

While at the store, I ran into Jason's cousin Liz. Now, don't get me wrong, Liz is one of the nicest people on the planet. She's sweet. She's funny. She's thoughtful. She's also incredibly chatty. After twenty minutes of being brought up to speed on every aspect of her children's lives right down to the tint of her daughter's contact lenses, I told her I had to get to work and we went our separate ways so I could now go pee because I had to go again.

It turns out those over the counter medications only take the edge off the symptoms long enough to make you not suicidal from the pain. I called my doctor's office at 1:30 to see if they could either squeeze me in or simply be kind enough to call in a prescription for those wonderful pills to make the pain stop. The entire office was at lunch. Great. On my way home that afternoon, I called the office back to see if they could squeeze me in or if I should just go to the ER. The kind woman on the phone took pity on me and said if I was OK with not seeing a practitioner of medicine and just wanted to go to the lab to pee in a cup, she would authorize it and depending on the results, she would call in the prescription for me. That sounded like an excellent plan. I went to the lab, peed in a cup and went home to wait for her to call.

An hour later, I received that call to determine that I had a "rip roaring infection" and she was calling in the prescription for the antibiotics that would make the world right again. I peed before I left, but since the drive was 20 minutes to the pharmacy, I had to pee again by the time I got there. I was practically bouncing by the time I made it to the bathroom that was conveniently located in the back of the store. I was trying desperately to take my pants off without peeing myself and jumping up and down that I didn't notice the poop on the toilet seat. Yup, I sat in poop. Even as I type this, I want to go take a shower because that's a level of gross I just can't handle. However, I was able to find my happy thought as I was mere feet away from my magic pills, so I bought another bottle of cranberry juice, popped the first pill, went home to go take a scalding shower in bleach and waited for sweet relief to kick in.

The next day, Wednesday, the meds had started working their magic and I was in good spirits even though Aurora was going to have surgery that day. Aurora was scheduled for her second surgery in the span two weeks to fix the abscess that had formed in the root of one of her molars. About four weeks prior to this day, Aurora's nose had started bleeding. Not a significant amount of blood, just a small steady stream, enough to probably be annoying for her and to set my panic into overdrive. Clearly she had a brain tumor or was going to have an aneurysm at any moment. What else could it be? Dr. Dutton assured me, as did Dr. Barlow, the world was still going to continue to revolve around the sun, she had a mere tooth root abscess. A tooth root abscess is an infection at the stem of the tooth. The cure is to surgically remove the tooth, let the infected fluids that have surrounded the tooth drain, and follow a ten day course of antibiotics.

Dr. Dutton is one of the most forward thinking veterinarians I have ever known. He truly has all the cutting edge equipment before it's mainstream. Aurora's arthritis had started taking its toll. Stairs were quickly becoming an issue. Despite the underwater treadmill therapy she was getting with Joyce, she was in a substantial amount of pain. Dr. Dutton and Dr. Barlow were now officially licensed to perform stem cell therapy in dogs and cats.

I did a ton of research. It was amazing to read the results of animals that were facing euthanasia due to immobility that were returned to juvenile status through the stem cell therapy. I had asked several people their thoughts and we received the green light reviews from Dr. Ham who sees the benefits every day with horses. Aurora is a small pony to most so score 1. Joyce, Aurora's physical therapist, has been chomping at the bit for someone in our area to do this procedure because is has such amazing results, again Score 2. Finally, I was doing a lesson package for a veterinarian and even she said stem cell therapy is the way to go for arthritis care. The third time was the charm and we looked forward to taking Aurora on longer walks with us and the rest of the stooges.

The way it works is the pet is anesthetized to collect fat cells. The fat cells are then sent to a lab and broken down to the stem cells. The stem cells are then injected back into the animal and they go to work to repair damaged tissue, ligaments, muscles, bones, and organs… You name it those little stem cells fix it.

So, we decided while she had the surgery for her tooth, we would also have the doctor perform the stem cell procedure. Within <u>TWELVE HOURS</u> of her recovery we had our girl back. She was bounding around like a puppy. She was following me everywhere. I went upstairs and she followed me. I went back downstairs and she was right there. I went outside and she was right behind me. I even got a rather frantic call from Jason that Aurora, the girl who hadn't worn her Invisible Fence® collar in five years, yes, even I am that owner, (sorry Henry), had breached her system. That was a true testament to how well she was feeling. She hadn't gone anywhere near the boundaries after her training hence the lack of a collar for her containment. Rest assured though, Tatum and Porter have their batteries changed in their collars every 90 days without fail. Trust them I don't.

The stem cell procedure is expensive and we are still paying for it, but for the relief it gave her, I would do it one hundred more times without question. I need to be able to look at myself in the mirror when I say I've done everything I could for the care of my dogs. It's just money.

Two weeks passed after the first surgery to remove the tooth and stem cell therapy, and while her mobility remained unfettered, the swelling in her face hadn't gone down the way it was supposed to and her eye was now swollen shut. The doctor thinks the pus pocket that had formed under her eye due to the first infection had closed up before all the pus had drained and essentially, the wound reabscessed.

That Wednesday, the day after the painful potty bleeding had started for me, she had another surgery and Dr. Dutton went back in to her cheek. This time, he cut a hole in her cheek and placed a drain from her cheek to the hole in her mouth where her tooth used to be so it could have a better route to drain blood and yuck all over my house. The doctor also ordered a test to culture her infected fluids to see what was causing the second abscess.

Oh, she was the picture of pathetic after that second surgery. She was crying, whimpering, and just a very sad little girl. I knew I needed to get ahead of her pain, so I gave her the same sedative I accidentally took last winter and just waited for the good effects to kick in. They never did.

At 3:00 in the morning, she really started crying in pain. I got up to lay with her on the floor and comfort her. With Aurora, just being with her and holding her paw was usually enough to calm her down so she would go back to sleep and within 15 minutes, I was often able to resume my position nestled between my sheets snuggled with Jason or my teddy bear. Just as I was about to fall back to sleep with Aurora, Porter assumed it was time to get up and Killian also got up informed me he had to go potty that very minute. I grumpily got up and brought the dogs that wanted to go potty outside. Upon returning to the bedroom, Aurora was now "up" because the term standing would require she had a semblance of balance, which she did not. Jason made some comment about what she needed that now I can't even recall, but I do remember snarling at him that was not her problem, I put her and everyone else on their beds and threatened the next being that awoke me, be it two or four legged, with death. I got back on the floor with Aurora and fell back to sleep.

The drain wasn't doing what it was supposed to because by the time I got home from work on Saturday, three days later, she looked like a golf ball had lodged in her cheek, her eye was swollen shut again, her third eyelid was totally exposed, and now she had the foul stench of death about her. We had received a preliminary report on the culture: the first round of antibiotics were ineffective to her infection so basically, the infection was able to rage inside her because the medicine wasn't suited for the infection she had. Oh, and the source of said infection was e Coli. Just good times had by all. However, the new antibiotics showed to be appropriate for the infection. Of course they were, a ten day supply was $150. After hemming and hawing, I decided I would sleep better if she were seen by a veterinary professional because bad smells do in fact equal bad things. Back to the ER we went since it was now 7:00 on a Saturday night.

Aurora had a slight temperature of 102.8. The staff was able to flush out the wound, which I guess was pretty nasty with bloody gross chunks all in it. We were sent home with another prescription to supplement the current medication as well as a syringe so I could flush the wound at home as well as instructions to put a hot compress on the wound as often as possible. I'm not squeamish, so bring on the blood and guts.

The following day, we started flushing in earnest to help our little girl. For grins, I took her temperature, which was now at 103.6. A little concerning but I'm not hitting the panic button yet. However, now she was starting to walk away from her food. Aurora will sell her soul for a Dorito. In five years, that dog has never, ever walked away from food. In fact, we had to install an indoor unit for the Invisible Fence® to keep her from jumping on the counter and stealing *our* food. But again, she's got a nasty hole that's draining blood in her mouth; it is possibly feasible that any other dog might not want to eat. However, I was feeding her *the good stuff.* She was getting canned salmon. Oh, and she still stunk of rotting flesh.

I called the ER back to update them on the elevated temperature and the decreased appetite and basically, my plan was to bring her in for observation and flushing at the Weare Animal Hospital the following day, but I wanted to know if there was anything I could or should do in the meantime to make her more comfortable and if there were any other signs that could indicate a bad thing? I was told no and just keep an eye on her.

Jason and I discussed our options for the following day. He was leaving for Indiana the next morning. His flight was at 9:00. The animal hospital opens at 7:30. I had to leave the house at 7:00 so I could make it to my first call on time in a suburb of Boston. He agreed to drop her off and hope he wouldn't miss his flight. Since he wasn't checking any luggage, we were confident he would be fine.

Monday, her temperature is 103.6 again, she's still walking away from food, and yup, there's that familiar disgusting odor coming from our dog. Jason brought her to the hospital and made his flight without a problem. I called the animal hospital for an update around 11, and flushing had commenced fine, it was clear Aurora felt like crap, but she was stable and all things considered, doing well. I called my mother because I needed her to go get Aurora and bring her home that evening since my last call was at 3:45 and it was an hour away in Andover Massachusetts and if there was traffic or a delay, I needed someone to go get Big Mama, not to mention I had to get everyone fed and go to obedience class with Porter, dogs on the side of the road be damned this week… No, they wouldn't, but perhaps it wouldn't be an issue I hoped to myself.

Tuesday, her temperature was 104. Oh, that's not good. Not good at all. I also had to wrap her medication in turkey in order to get her to take them because she was refusing the canned food. However, Jason is out of town and again, and I need to leave at 7:00 in order to make it to my first appointment on time. I fed everyone else, put them in their crates, and left for what was going to be a long, worry filled day.

I called Jason on my way to my appointment with an update and for the first time, I heard panic in his voice regarding Aurora. He was surprised and I could tell somewhat annoyed I didn't cancel my first call to bring her in for another day of observation and urged to the point of demanded me to have someone go get her and bring her in for another examination and flushing. I called my Dad. I forgot he was out of town. I called my brother. He was in Vermont at a job site. My mom was at work and already scrubbed in for a surgery. I called Maureen to get the phone number of a local woman, Joy, who owns Peace of Mind Pet Sitting Service. She agreed to go get Aurora and bring her to the vet's within a couple hours. Jason was satisfied with that news.

Joy called me twice. She called me and left me a voicemail when she picked up Aurora and was driving down our driveway leaving the house. Even though Aurora was oozing blood and slobbering drool on Joy's shoulder on the commute, Joy knew Aurora needed her and she was happy to do her part. She left another message after she dropped off Aurora at the hospital. Her voice was shaking with worry. I had also noted the worry in Maureen's voice at the news of Aurora's condition. Dog people just *get it.* Because dogs can't talk, we can't truly know the level of their discomfort. In Aurora's case, she's so darn stoic for her to exhibit anything clearly means she's in distress. There was a collective silent prayer being said by many people for Aurora's recovery.

The report was similar when I called the vet that afternoon for an update. Flushing is going well, she feels like crap, but we are playing a game of patience. We agreed as long as she has a fever, it is in her best interest she be observed and this will also allow for more frequent flushing of her wound because, according to Dr. Dutton, "The solution to pollution is dilution." When I picked Aurora up that afternoon, I overheard the staff in the back room talking about how good Aurora is as a patient and how sorry they are she feels so lousy. It's kind of a heartwarming feeling when your dog holds a special place in the hearts of everyone she meets.

Wednesday, she still had a temperature of 104, and she was still refusing to eat. I was in tears when I brought her into the hospital that morning for more observation and flushing before I started my workday. I was exhausted. I was frustrated. I just wanted this ordeal to be over for the big girl. The schedule gods at work were not taking pity on me and for some reason; the suburbs of Boston had become my territory that week. Sure, I was getting paid for drive time for the excessive commutes, but at this point, I was in a position where I felt like I had to choose between my dog and my job and I was burning out quickly. I had to call my brother to ask him to leave his own job early so he could go get Aurora because my last call was an hour and a half away and oh gee, I'd be hitting Route 95 traffic in Boston at 5:00. I didn't have a hope in Hades of getting home before 7:00 and the clinic closed at 6:00. The staff was being wonderful to me. They always are, don't get me wrong, and Aurora is kind of a staff favorite, so they were keenly aware how upset I was and they were doing everything they could to make our lives easier.

The doctors added another antibiotic on top of the one she was already getting, plus the medication she was still on from the emergency room doctor. To quote Dr Dutton: "Research shows that the combination of these meds will hopefully knock the stuffing out of the infection and reduce the fever." Sure. The flushing was still going well. And, according to the doctors and staff, perhaps Aurora didn't like my food because she was chowing down on their Science Diet food like it was the last supper.

I don't want to sound like an ingrate here, she's eating and I'm thrilled. But *come on*! Science Diet? My dogs get the top shelf, best of the best, crème de la crème for food. Science Diet, at best, is a medium grade food with more preservatives and additives than I prefer to feed my dogs. I will concede since the dog food scare, Science Diet and many other foods that are of medium quality have switched their menus to include more whole foods and less byproducts and preservatives. That being said, I went directly to the pet store on my way home and got a more appropriate food for her. It had two ingredients: Chicken and water. No fillers. No preservatives. No additives. Chicken. Water. That's it. However, to prove how much she liked their food and not so much the food I got her, they sent me a picture of her in her cage. The bowl of salmon I sent with her was still full and untouched. However, she was literally wrapped around their food bowl and snarfing down every last crumb she could find. Showoffs.

My brother texted me to say he had gotten Big Mama. He used my truck to get her since his has no shocks whatsoever. My truck, the Jimmy, has become the dog vehicle. It stinks. It has hair and dirt everywhere. Denali threw up in it. Tatum peed in it. It's gross. But, it's the dog vehicle. What do you expect? Mike also noted my truck was a nice little rig. It stinks of skank, he said, but that he liked it. Oh, and Aurora also has quite the funky odor about her as well. Family. Who else can help you and insult you at the same time?

Finally, on Thursday Aurora's fever broke. It was 101.7. We did the dance of joy. She ate her entire breakfast of chicken and water. There was more rejoicing. There was pep in her step. Again, hark the herald Angels sing. We decided that the flushing should continue at the hospital and they were all fine with that. I updated everyone on the good news. We all breathed a collective sigh of relief. However, I was spent. Absolutely drained.

I arrived early to a customer's house that afternoon. She wasn't home yet. I parked in her driveway under a tree and fell asleep reading a book. I never heard the customer drive past my car when she got home. When she woke me up by standing at the window, I was the picture of... Well, I was a mess. There was drool on my face and my whole leg had fallen asleep so I was unable to move for five minutes for fear of collapsing. Normally, I try to put on an energetic performance of fun and squeak to engage the dog to frolic and gauge the dog's understanding of its boundaries. Not this time. Throwing the ball was a stretch for me. Nonetheless, we determined the dog was well trained to the Invisible Fence®, I yawned, thanked her, yawned again, and set about my two hour ride home.

The following week, the bloody discharge, which had dissipated, was back in full force and her cheek was swollen again despite continued flushing. I called the Weare Animal Hospital to make an appointment for her. It was a Wednesday and Dr. Dutton was there on his day off to do some bookkeeping and did a drive by exam of Aurora to which he concluded she had, by far, the worst tooth root abscess he had ever seen and while she is recovering, it is at time warping snail speed. I asked him if it was time to start thinking scary things. He basically told me I could, but he would bet anything all she had was inflamed tissue due to chronic infection. Fret not young grasshopper. I left Aurora for the day for the staff to continue the flushing. Why get my floors dirty if I don't have to?

However, his young Padawan Jedi To Be Dr. Barlow called me later that afternoon. She had flipped open Aurora's mouth and noticed significant tissue growth around the tooth removal site. Similar to Dr. Dutton's thoughts, she felt fairly confident it was just inflamed tissue due to chronic infection. But, since tissue growths in mouths are usually bad things, she said she needed to be able to sleep at night when she told me my dog didn't have cancer and did a biopsy, just to be sure.

Aurora was a true champ for the biopsy. Even Dr. Barlow was amazed at how well Aurora handled having a chunk of her gum removed from her mouth without anesthesia, sedative, or even a piece of cheese. We all threw up every day while waiting for the results. We were all thinking good thoughts but growths in mouths are never a good thing. It had possibly been the longest, and perhaps the worst three weeks I had endured in a long time.

I was very touched by the outpouring of support from my friends and family. My coworkers would e mail every morning for progress reports. My mom and dad would send supportive e mails asking about her condition. My brother would text me for updates. Maureen and Joy were calling for updates and a shoulder on which for me to lean. My friend Jen was sending reiki to Aurora and me help us. Even Aurora's physical therapist was thinking good thoughts for us. It's not very often I feel blessed, but it is a very heart warming feeling to know how much people care about you, but more importantly, genuinely care about your dog.

The following Monday morning at 6:15, Aurora had a seizure. It was short, only twenty seconds. But that clearly changed the playing field. The last seizure she had was at 3:30 AM two years prior. Most idiopathic seizures, or ones that occur for no real reason, occur from midnight to 2:00 AM. Something was clearly not right with her. She was still bleeding like a siv; even her eye boogers now had a red tinge to them, and now this.

I was in the kitchen making coffee for the day mulling over the situation. The last seizure she had was close to within the normal range of when random seizures occur. But what if this isn't a random seizure? What if she has another one when no one is home? I didn't want to press the panic button but what if there was another seizure and no one was there to help her? It was pure luck that we even knew she had one. Jason was getting into the shower and I was about to go downstairs with the other stooges to let them out for potty. All of a sudden, Aurora shot off her bed and was standing by the dresser swaying back and forth. When it occurred to me what was happening, I wrapped around her and yelled to Jason to turn on the lights.

"The hall light is on," he stated.

"SHE'S HAVING A SEIZURE. TURN ON THE DAMN LIGHT!!!!" I yelled.

Had this happened twenty seconds later, no one would have known. Jason brought her in for more observation that day. He met Dr. Dutton in the parking lot. Dr. Dutton was on his way to check the mail and cheerily asked "Is she spending the day with us again?"

"Yeah, she had a seizure an hour ago."

According to Jason, you could have hit him with a feather and it would have knocked him over. His head just dropped. He had no explanation. Almost a hint of defeat.

"Well," he sighed, "if this was anyone else's dog, I'd be surprised. Bring her on in."

The usual 11:00 check in report was positive. Aurora hadn't had a seizure since that morning. She was distressed because there was a dog in the cage next to her that was having a hard recovery from her spay surgery, and another dog that was hurting from his ACL surgery and she clearly just wanted to mother them. But she was fine. No word from the lab on the biopsy yet. However, the lab had called with another dog's results and the doctor updated them on Aurora's situation and asked that special care be given to get those results back *as soon as humanly possible.*

At 6:00, Dr. Dutton called me at home from his home; that is never a good sign.

"Hey, it's Mike." There wasn't a hint of cheer in his voice.

"Hi."

"I got the biopsy report back."

"Is it time to start thinking scary thoughts?" I kind of joked, but totally praying for good news.

"Yeah. Yeah it is. It's squamous cell carcinoma."

I collapsed onto the floor. Squamous cell carcinoma for dogs that has festered in the mouth is basically a death sentence. By the time it is discovered the chances of beating it are very small. In Aurora's case, it would be just plain cruel to consider chemotherapy, radiation, or anything else but letting her go with the dignity in which she always lived. The doctor felt the time to make some quality of life issues was looming in the near future and she was probably in considerable discomfort.

Jason was working late and wouldn't be home for at least two hours. I wasn't going to call him at work because he still wouldn't be able to leave and he would have to work knowing 1. his little girl was dying and we couldn't save her and 2. I was a sobbing fool at home. And I was. I was curled in a ball on the floor, sobbing, processing the end of the Aurora Era. My Big Girl. Big Mama. My rock. My stability. My protector. What the hell was I going to do now without her?

I called Maureen. No answer. I called two more times. No answer. Well I couldn't deal with this alone and there was a long list of people I needed to notify. I called my mom. I have to say when

I'm upset and cranky, she isn't going to offer more than a "get over it." But when there is a substantial source of pain and grief, she is an amazing source of support. Even her voice shook with sadness at the upcoming and inevitable loss of Mama.

Then a spat ensued about easing Rora's suffering sooner rather than later. She felt my day off was Wednesday, two days from that moment, and that was a good opportunity to ease her suffering. We went a few rounds before I snapped, "She's my dog. It's my decision and I still haven't told Jason. She's his little girl too." She relented. Two days later she called to see how things were going. I gave her the update to let her know the following Monday, Aurora would be sent on her way to join Denali and the ferrets. I swear to Christmas I am the person she created.

"Well, don't hold on to her too long for your sake. Or for me that matter."

"Mom, I thought you were offing yourself the day you can't find your glasses and you discover you're wearing them."

"I am."

"Well then we're all set."

I called Maureen and we cried together. Despite everything, Maureen knows Mama didn't mean it when Aurora bit her. Maureen is also intensely aware my sense of self due to Aurora's proximity. She is a firm believer in lessons we learn from life. I begged her for a hint as to what in the name of everything the universe wants me to learn. She opted to let me determine my own lesson from Denali's loss, which I still don't know. But to lose both my protectors within a 16 month span, or so I had so relinquished said title, she told me its time to stand on my own. I can take care of myself.

I called Dad, the original protector. His sobbing daughters were never his strong point. Couple that with the loss of a dog and he checked out. Growing up, when we lost our dogs due to illness, Dad could never go for the last appointment and he reminded me he would have traded us kids for those moments when we were losing a furry family member. When I was in college, we had a Belgian Malinois that we had rescued that *hated* women. His name was Sam. He was handsome. He was smart. He was Dad's pal. He died because of me. I was home for the summer from college and it was pretty clear he was going to hurt me when I would come home late from work or a date. Dad ached over the loss of Sam. I think of all the dogs we had growing up, Sam was *his* dog; all the others had been Mom's dogs. Sound familiar? Dad was sad for me. He knew the intensity of my passion for my dogs. He was at the lake the previous summer and witnessed my powerful disgust for another's insensitivity to the situation when it was suggested I just take Denali out back and shoot him to save some money. Dad offered his condolences and the usual if I need anything, just call.

I called my brother and one of my coworkers. They heard the crack in my voice and they both had the same response, "NO!" Everyone that met Aurora loved her. So I made the calls, sent out the e mails, and just waited for Jason to get home.

By all accounts, Jason is a rock. He keeps his emotions on the inside. We discussed the situation, the options, and agreed it was in her best interest to send her on her way with the dignity and grace with which she lived. The following week was hurry up and wait. While we didn't want to rush the end, we also wanted to just get the inevitable over with and start the grieving process. I took a peek in her mouth to see the mass that raised Dr. Barlow's suspicions and saw the monster that was killing her. The tumor was growing at a rapid pace and it was an angry looking beast. It had grown to the size of my thumb and had gray, green, and purple bumps on it. We had a ferret named Ryker that was having difficulty breathing. X rays revealed a mass in his chest. Surgery revealed a nasty tumor running through his heart. The tumor in Aurora's mouth was very similar. At first we thought the seizure was a sign the tumor had spread to her brain. Due to the lack of any seizures thereafter, we think it was a sign to us to just let her go without heroics.

We made plans for the weekend to make it All About Aurora. We bought steak for her, made her scrambled eggs. He made her a stew. We picked up apples to make her some applesauce. Jason also threw in some vodka and made us a couple drinks to take the edge off what was quickly becoming a countdown. We went to the ice cream stand and watched her get a brain freeze as she licked every last drop of creamy vanilla ice cream. We took her for a walk but it was pretty clear she felt rotten so Jason continued the walk with the other three stooges and Rora and I just sat and enjoyed the foliage.

Jason made an amazing breakfast for Aurora's last meal. He made it his mission that week to cram in as much love and happiness for her as he could before she was gone forever. He made her scrambled eggs with cheese. Tripe. Blended Haddock. She was in her glory getting all these yummy meals. But she was ready. She was tired of being sick. And on the front steps, sitting on her bed with blankets, where she spent many years overseeing her kingdom, we sent her on her way.

I believe in letting all members of the family in on the information the pack number has changed. After the doctor left, we let the dogs out, one by one, to confirm Aurora's passing. Killian was more concerned with me and wouldn't leave my side even to sniff her. Tatum came bounding out and raced to her and sniffed her mouth. Porter seemed most affected. He would sniff her, then he would come to me and nudge me then look over at her with a "Well, go fix her" look on his face. The UPS man then came down the driveway so we put everyone that was barking inside. After he left, that's when it hit Tatum something was very different with Aurora.

She sniffed her in earnest. Porter tried snuggling with her but kept a paw on my leg to make sure I wasn't going anywhere.

On Wednesday, Porter spent the morning looking for Aurora. I told him in this instance, she isn't coming back and someday he would see her again. That evening, Porter was in the dog room and every so often I would hear an exasperated sigh. Finally, I peeked in to check on him and there he was, in Aurora's crate. His ears were pinned and his eyes were so wide, so empty, so lost. He was so sad. They grieve too.

The next day, he and Tatum were in day care. Porter was there to have fun. Tatum was there to get her butt kicked to keep her status of Reigning Imp in check. Without Aurora, the change in pack paradigm was going to be a force with which to reckon. Jason and I agreed we would always find the money to continue the Tatum Butt Kicking Daycare. As it turned out, Porter was the one who needed the most canine interaction as he decided he would try to bully his way into the alpha position. He even growled at Killian while we were all on the bed snuggling one Sunday morning and I launched him across the room and explained to him in no uncertain terms I love Killian more than I love Jason. Jason backed me up and said, "It's true Buddy. And if she wants to nuke you for hurting Killian, I will be powerless to stop it."

Again, our eternal gratitude goes out to the doctors and staff at the Weare Animal Hospital. Their unwavering and eternal patience was without question what kept us sane. We also cannot thank the folks at Angel View Pet Cemetery for their compassion, especially Mike, who made such a nice pillow for Aurora's head with her blanket as he laid her to rest for us to say goodbye. Lastly, the following days of friends and family checking in to see how we were doing was most heartwarming. While the sadness is real and the emptiness in our house can be deafening, with Aurora we have closure. We never really got that closure with Denali because it was an unconfirmed diagnosis. With Denali, we had an over-powering sense of defeat because we couldn't fix what was wrong because we simply didn't know. With Aurora, while it would have been real nice to have more than a week to process her illness, at least we knew it was a battle she couldn't win. Rest in peace Big Mama. Rest in peace.

# Afterward

When I started this book almost a year ago, I was following the pattern of John Grogan's Marley and Me just telling little anecdotes about the chaos that comes from living with four dogs. I've read his book several times and giggle at the similarities of bedlam that run through our houses. Conversely, I was writing the book as things occurred, not after the fact. I never dreamed, though, that one of my characters would leave me while I was still writing the book. So while I'm sure my life and the characters with whom I share my little section of earth will continue to provide stories that make you say, "Oh Good Lord," and continue to question my sanity and ability to cope in public unsupervised, telling those stories without Aurora doesn't seem right.

Made in the USA
Lexington, KY
26 November 2011